PROLEGOMENA TO CHARITY

PERSPECTIVES IN CONTINENTAL PHILOSOPHY
John D. Caputo, series editor

1. John D. Caputo, ed., *Deconstruction in a Nutshell: A Conversation with Jacques Derrida.*
2. Michael Strawser, *Both/And: Reading Kierkegaard—From Irony to Edification.*
3. Michael Barber, *Ethical Hermeneutics: Rationality in Enrique Dussel's Philosophy of Liberation.*
4. James H. Olthuis, ed., *Knowing Other-wise: Philosophy at the Threshold of Spirituality.*
5. James Swindal, *Reflection Revisited: Jürgen Habermas's Discursive Theory of Truth.*
6. Richard Kearney, *Poetics of Imagining: Modern and Postmodern.* Second edition.
7. Thomas W. Busch, *Circulating Being: From Embodiment to Incorporation—Essays on Late Existentialism.*
8. Edith Wyschogrod, *Emmanuel Levinas: The Problem of Ethical Metaphysics.* Second edition.
9. Francis J. Ambrosio, ed., *The Question of Christian Philosophy Today.*
10. Jeffrey Bloechl, ed., *The Face of the Other and the Trace of God: Essays on the Philosophy of Emmanuel Levinas.*
11. Ilse N. Bulhof and Laurens ten Kate, eds., *Flight of the Gods: Philosophical Perspectives on Negative Theology.*
12. Trish Glazebrook, *Heidegger's Philosophy of Science.*
13. Kevin Hart, *The Trespass of the Sign.* Second edition.
14. Mark C. Taylor, *Journeys to Selfhood: Hegel and Kierkegaard.* Second edition.
15. Dominique Janicaud, Jean-François Courtine, Jean-Louis Chrétien, Michel Henry, Jean-Luc Marion, and Paul Ricoeur, *Phenomenology and the "Theological Turn": The French Debate.*
16. Karl Jaspers, *The Question of German Guilt.* Introduction by Joseph W. Koterski, S.J.
17. Jean-Luc Marion, *The Idol and Distance: Five Studies.* Translated with an introduction by Thomas A. Carlson.
18. Jeffrey Dudiak, *The Intrigue of Ethics: A Reading of the Idea of Discourse in the Thought of Emmanuel Levinas.*
19. Robyn Horner, *Rethinking God As Gift: Marion, Derrida, and the Limits of Phenomenology.*
20. Mark Dooley, *The Politics of Exodus: Søren Kierkegaard's Ethic of Responsibility.*
21. Merold E. Westphal, Jr., *Overcoming Onto-theology: Toward a Postmodern Christian Faith.*
22. Stanislas Breton, *The Word and the Cross.* Translated with an introduction by Jacquelyn Porter.
23. Edith Wyschogrod, Jean-Joseph Goux, and Eric Boynton, eds. *The Enigma of Gift and Sacrifice.*

Prolegomena to Charity

JEAN-LUC MARION

Translated by STEPHEN E. LEWIS

Fordham University Press
New York
2002

Copyright © 2002 by Fordham University Press
Originally published as *Prolégomènes à la charité* © E.L.A. La
Différence, Paris, 1986

Perspectives in Continental Philosophy, No. 24
ISSN 1089–3938

Library of Congress Cataloging-in-Publication Data
available

Printed in the United States of America
02   03   04   05   06   5   4   3   2   1
First Edition

To J.-R. Bradurion

CONTENTS

FOREWORD TO THE AMERICAN TRANSLATION

> . . . love, perfect and reinvented measure, marvelous and unforeseen reason . . .
>
> Arthur Rimbaud[1]

WE ALL THINK we know a good deal, or at least enough, about love, if only because, in the final analysis, we live, breathe, and *are* in it. For everything in our world, when its daily actuality reduces to what, in the end, it truly gives us, is summed up by questions of love and hate. But this atmosphere permeates us so originally that we question ourselves in only a very mediocre fashion about its uneasy primacy. The tendency is to conclude that because love goes without saying, it therefore goes along without us. At our best, we keep an eye on it at a distance, as long as we are able to remain outside its reach; and only if we find ourselves forced by the tumult of passions do we go and take a closer look. But at our normal cruising speed we have neither the need nor the urgency to think love, to question it, to respond to it. Love, like youth, must pass away. And if, nevertheless, we must speak of it, the popular song always seems more adequate than the best novels. Soon, everything falls back into order—nothing more to say of love, nothing more to expect from it.

Like most wastelands, this wasteland of love is in no way natural—it is the result of our decision, or at least our inertia.

---

[1] Arthur Rimbaud, *Œuvres Complètes, Illuminations,* "Génie," ed. A. Rolland de Renéville (Paris: Pléiade, 1963), p. 205.

For if we say nothing, or very little, of love, if love speaks to us and says so very little, it is because we hardly understand what it says and how it speaks. In fact, love remains nearly unintelligible to us, because its rigor (and whoever has experienced it once knows how frightfully well it can imprison us) eludes us most of the time. How can what is closest to us become so foreign? In fact, love does not lack rationality. But its rationality unfolds in paradoxes, which elude the most quotidian rationality, the calculations and measurements of technology that are sufficient for constituting the world's objects. Love obeys a reason—a reason that, nevertheless, deals not with objects but with those, like you and I, who handle them, occasionally produce them, and are ever using them for ambitions other than those posted by their obvious finalities. What do you think of, reader, when you read? Not of this book, nor even of what I want to tell you (surely not of love as an academic subject, neutral and restrained for the sake of an elevated discussion), but rather of whether, one day, you will succeed in loving and being loved, and whether or not this book might help you. Behind and through objects, you do not think of them; on the contrary, you think of only one thing—saying love, in order to be able to make it, and making charity, too, in order to succeed in saying it. And we immediately feel that this intention follows a logic that is completely different from the logic overseeing the management and arrangement of objects.

Love deploys the rationality of those who stage objectivity without entering into it, the actors acted by and acting through their final desire—to love and to be loved. Love treats only of the reason of loving and of making oneself loved: as long as we refuse to enter into this tautology, we inevitably degrade love to a metaphor of relation with objects (possession, production, conquest, consumption, and so on), and thereby miss it completely. In order to enter into the tautology of love, we must risk following several paradoxes. But paradoxes do not put reason into question; on the contrary, they secure for reason its most unshakable supports.

The studies that follow[2] do not claim to describe these paradoxes in every detail, and even less to allow the question of charity to emerge from an axiomatic of love. Difficulty here discourages the most self-assured force of mind. As in the first French edition of this collection (1986), the ambition here is only to trace several prolegomena to the question of love and of charity. Prolegomena, or what one is able to say when one is not yet able to say it outright: leveling the hills, straightening the paths, clearing the obstacles. There should be no surprise, then, that these preparatory labors venture wherever the possibility of a discovery may lie, moving without reticence away from the territory of familiar philosophy in order to traverse phenomenology as well as the most straightforwardly christological theology. For in order to reach love, we must neither favor certain disciplines over others, nor close the few doors we find open.

Since the publication of the first edition, I have attempted, particularly in *Etant donné: Essai d'une phénoménologie de la donation* (Paris: Presses Universitaires de France, 1997, 1998; American translation by Jeffrey L. Kosky, Stanford University Press, 2002), to lay down more than prolegomena—to sketch the phenomenological situation of an *ego* for whom, at the very outset and on principle, loving and being loved is not forbidden. This *ego*, designated as he who is given over to the phenomenon *(l'adonné au phénomène)*, and himself thought from donation as point of departure, can in effect expose himself to an *alter ego*, who does not reduce to his object, because this alter ego comes to him, without cause, without expectation, and contrary to all intentionality. But the possibility thus opened for a conceptual approach to love has not yet been pursued nor brought to conclusion. While waiting to keep the promises that I have dared to make, I would like at least to render a service: to regain, concerning

---

[2] I thank the *Revue catholique internationale Communio*, Editions Verdier, the Librairie Arthème Fayard, and the journal *Autrement* for allowing me to take up here the first version of certain texts and to rework them extensively. In this translation, I add a seventh study.

love (and thus charity), several evidences that have most often been lost in the spectral clarity of the world's objects.

I am happy to thank John D. Caputo for having welcomed this book, along with others, into his series; Stephen E. Lewis for having skillfully translated it; and the American public, for its openness of spirit and readiness to receive.

J.-L. M.
December 1999

TRANSLATOR'S ACKNOWLEDGMENTS

I WOULD LIKE to thank Jeffrey L. Kosky for sharing with me his rough draft of a translation of this book and Jean-Luc Marion for his helpful answers to numerous queries. I also want to express my gratitude to the Lumen Christi Institute for the spirited Catholic intellectual climate it fosters at the University of Chicago and beyond. Finally, to my companions in all I do—Suzanne, Sophie, Simone, and Serena—I give thanks and recognition for boundless love and support.

1

Evil in Person

The devil follows me day and night, because he is
afraid to be alone.

Francis Picabia

IN ORDER TO ARRIVE at the one who concentrates the "mystery of iniquity" in himself (2 Thessalonians 2:7), it makes
sense to sketch iniquity, at least in outline. For iniquity
spreads forth a rigorous injustice, ordered and irremediably
logical. Evil would not destroy us so thoroughly if it did not
destroy us with such logic. In the experience of evil, what,
in a sense, hurts the most *(fait le plus mal)*[1] results from the
indisputable rigor iniquity deploys. Iniquity is not characterized by any absurdity, any incoherence, nor even by any "injustice" (in the everyday sense of an unfair wage, or an effect
disproportionate to its cause). Rather, it is characterized only
by an immutable logic that reproduces its rigor without end
or flaw, to the point of nausea, according to an insurmountable boredom. But one dies of boredom, too, especially of
boredom. The logic of iniquity will thus lead us to its mystery, and to what it implies in the end.

REVENGE

Before all else, evil hurts. Whether suffering affects me physically or morally, it imposes itself with pain, as a pain. Evil is

---

[1] [Translator's note: This essay plays on the fact that, in French, "to
hurt" and "to do evil" are both rendered by the expression *faire mal,*
which is similar to the (nowadays somewhat archaic) English expression
"to do ill." Accordingly, the reader should try throughout this text to hear
the evil in every mention of hurt, and vice versa.]

experienced as the only indisputable fact, short of all delusion, that is exempt from the need for any proof or argument. The evil that hurts me never deceives. This pain, as I undergo it, necessitates my reacting to it in order to free myself from it; thus, even my struggle against suffering, in the very moment when I am attempting to deliver myself from its sting, proceeds, like a passion, from the evil I undergo. For if evil's first effect is suffering, its second is the demand that the suffering cease, at any price and at once. How? By suppressing the cause of the suffering. And yet, it remains necessary to find a cause. Or, more exactly, the immediate concern lies not in finding this cause but in suppressing it. To require its suppression does not first require the identification of the cause of the suffering. The certain, adequate, and presumably scientific knowledge of the cause often seems neither possible nor even desirable, the immediate concern being identification, without delay, of any interlocutor whatsoever. I am ignorant of the truth of the cause—but no matter, because I do know with certainty that I hurt, and that I can load my hurt onto somebody else. Even if I cannot identify this cause so as to annihilate it, I can plead it as mine. In contesting the perhaps unknown cause of my suffering, I plead my own cause, spontaneously and immediately. For evil, which appears to me only in its attack against me, calls for only one response—my own attack, intended to suppress it in return. Suppressing the cause of the evil amounts, first of all, to pleading my cause against it. At the least, the desire for revenge responds to each evil. The logic of evil thus puts forth its first necessity by arousing in me, who is suffering, the desire for another evil: to destroy the cause of the evil that is destroying me, to return to the evil its hurt, and to attack the attack; in short, to plead my own cause at any price, even before the cause of my injury is known.[2]

---

[2] No one has defined the spirit of revenge better than Nietzsche: "The spirit of revenge . . . : where there was suffering, one always wanted punishment too" (*Thus Spoke Zarathustra*, II, 20; *The Portable Nietzsche*, ed. Walter Kaufmann [New York: Penguin, 1982], p. 252); for "every suffer-

PLEADING ONE'S CAUSE

Objectively, the cause of evil can very well precede the evil I undergo. But in all truth, when I undergo evil, I suffer from a suffering that, as it drives me mad, plunges me into a subjectivity "without doors or windows," in which the only things that count are my suffering and whatever that suffering inspires in me and points out to me; in the incarcerating subjectivity of suffering, the priority of the cause of evil over its hurt is inverted: the experience of evil (*le mal ressenti*)—suffering—makes me frenetically plead my cause and thereby proclaim my innocence until, consequently, I furnish that experience of evil with an objective cause, after the fact, so as finally to attempt to suppress it. Subjectively pleading my cause, only later do I pursue a potential objective cause for my hurt. Thus the question becomes: What reality is it preferable to choose as the guilty cause against which I then may plead my innocence? Suffering, in pleading its innocence, can find itself a thousand different causes to destroy: the man who strikes and tortures me, the thief who robs me, but also the woman who ridicules me, the petty bureaucrat who stands in my way. The more suffering lasts and grows, the more I can and must find for it a precise and powerful cause. To do this, I can pass from one cause to the other, or even add them together, to the point of building—though only to the measure of what I suffer and endure—a multiform cause; thus institutionalized suffering legitimately has the right to

---

ing man instinctively seeks a cause for his suffering; more precisely, a doer; more definitely, a *guilty* doer, someone capable of suffering—in short, something living on which he can upon any pretext discharge his feelings, either in fact or *in effigie*" (*On the Genealogy of Morals* III:15, tr. Douglas Smith [Oxford: Oxford University Press, 1996], p. 105). But, and this is a decisive point, the logic of revenge is perhaps never surpassed by Nietzsche himself, inasmuch as the "actives" as well as the "passives" practice it; if the first alone escape from ressentiment ("spirit of revenge" in the strict sense), it is only insofar as they put to work "the real reaction, that of the deed" (*On the Genealogy of Morals* I:10, p. 22, and II:11, p. 56); certainly a lapse of time separates action and ressentiment, but both practice revenge.

find itself a cause that is also institutional. What matter, so long as innocent suffering—my own—can put a face to the cause of its suffering? To put a face to the cause of one's suffering is to be able, at once, to plead one's cause efficiently. I can only accuse a face, and the worst of sufferings consists precisely in not having any face to accuse. Anonymous suffering redoubles the evil (the hurt) because it prohibits the innocent from pleading his cause. Thus, as evil grows, the charges grow; and so, too, must grow the dignity (or the number) of the guilty. This is why collective and objective evil—today, malnutrition, unemployment, lack of knowledge as lack of power, political repression and the systematic contempt for human rights, and so on—gives rise to causes that, though collective, ideal, and diffuse (economic, political, ideological, etc.), do not, for all that, become anonymous: they keep a face, which those who plead against them rightly trace. We must not discredit this face too quickly, under the pretext that it quickly becomes a caricature; caricature draws its possibility only from highly identifiable and precise faces, which can be concentrated only because each of the oppressed knows them concretely: the class enemy, each time, has a name; the torturer, each time, has a name; the economic power that lays off or enlists, each time, has a name—a name that certainly fits it better than its proper name, and that is concentrated in an abhorred but nonetheless absolutely real name. Thus the cause plead by the sufferer identifies the cause of hurt, of his hurt. Paradoxically, therefore, to calm my innocence and to suppress the hurt in me, I begin first of all by recognizing it and concretizing it. Because for me, given up as I am to evil by suffering and by the logic of evil, deliverance comes through the destruction of the cause of evil, and because the destruction of the cause of evil first of all enjoins an accusation in which I plead my cause against the face of an accused, evil calls for a counter-evil. By a paradoxical but unavoidable logic, I can struggle against the evil that affects me only by affecting the world with an evil first reified, unveiled, and fixed by me. To rid myself (*me défaire*) of the evil in me, I must first make *(faire)* of it a not-me, that is to say, give birth to it—point it out to all the world, and thus put it in the world. If I (passively) undergo evil, it is actively that I kindle a counter-evil. And if the evil is universal, in me and around me—as, in fact, it clearly is—then the counter-evil of the accusation will have to become universal also. And in fact, the accusation does become universal. For accusation, obviously, offers itself as the final weapon of those who do not have, or no longer have, any other. But truly, must one own a weapon?

Unjust Innocence

This is where evil wins its first decisive victory: it compels the sufferer to maintain his innocence by an accusation, to perpetuate suffering through the demand for another suffering, to oppose evil with counter-evil. Obviously, there is no point in judging the sufferer—me, us, everyone—nor in giving the absurd advice to "do otherwise," for each of us knows that, left to our own devices, it becomes virtually impossible for us to "do otherwise." The severity of evil consists, precisely, in the way in which it imposes its logic on us as though it were the only logic feasible: our first effort at deliverance retains evil as its sole horizon. Counter-evil remains an evil, just as a backfire is still a fire—destructive, first and always. The triumph of the logic of evil within the very effort to be rid of it stands out markedly in the universal accusation. This phenomenon can take the following formulation: just because the cause of evil remains to me unknown, uncertain, and vague doesn't mean that I must give up trying to suppress it. Because my innocence suffers and will cease suffering only by suppressing a cause, the excess of suffering leads to an excess of accusation: the identity of the cause does not matter so long as I can identify a cause to suppress. In order to speak of such a cause, our time has invented expressions: "round up the usual suspects," but above all, "determine accountability." It is worth noting here that our time—that of nihilism—offers the remarkable distinction of furnishing a perfect (though not unexpected) support to the infinite demand for accusation: the essence of technology in effect qualifies man as potentially universally guilty, for it first of all defines him as the worker of the universe, the master and possessor of nature, and therefore the one responsible for the world. He is responsible for the world in all that he does—production as the practical disposition of the world, as if it were a capital to exploit—but also by what he does not do; for, by right, his mastery has neither limit nor condition: all that "is produced" without his having produced it, prior to or on the margins of his production (thus the protection of "nature," the notion of "natural" cataclysms), all that which man does not produce, is imposed on him by the essence of technology as something he must anticipate, and thus as something for which he is responsible. The farther man's knowledge extends (ideology, "human sciences," computer science, futurology), the more his universal responsibility proves correct. In this way, the essence of technology provides a decisive confirmation of the logic of evil: for every evil, there is always a cause: man.[3] Let us proceed from generic man to individuals, so as to formulate the fitting conclusion: it is always possible to find a guilty person worthy of accusation; any old innocent is good enough. There is good reason for this: this innocent is evidently an

---

[3] On universal accusation, see Rémi Brague, "Si ce n'est ton frère, c'est donc toi," *Revue catholique internationale Communio* II/4 (1977). One of the most exemplary literary figures of universal accusation, besides of course the work of Kafka (who describes it, however, only from the point of view of the accused), is found in Camus's *Caligula.* As emperor, Caligula receives absolute power, but as a man, an insurmountable suffering (the death of his mistress); he decides therefore to pursue the logic of revenge without reserve: "Logic, Caligula, follow where logic leads." Which implies first of all universal blame: "Let the accused come forward. I want my criminals, and they all are criminals. Bring in the condemned men. I must have my public. Judges, witnesses, accused—all sentenced to death without a hearing." Then comes self-accusation, the inevitable masterpiece of revenge: "Caligula! You, too; you, too, are guilty" (Albert Camus, *Caligula,* in *Théâtre, récits, nouvelles,* ed. R. Quillot [Paris: Pléiade, 1962], pp. 75, 28, 107; *Caligula and Three Other Plays,* tr. Stuart Gilbert [New York: Alfred A. Knopf, 1970], pp. 49, 17, 72).

innocent no longer; to be exact, only a real "innocent" could not have always already done evil; a common innocent, like this one, is not innocent: supposing that he isn't the precise cause of my present suffering, there is no doubt that he has been the cause of other sufferings, which others have endured thanks to him; by serving as the guilty one in the cause that my suffering pleads perhaps unjustly against him, he thus will ever only bear the counter-evil merited by an evil that he committed elsewhere. Next, if the innocent was, by extraordinary chance, authentically so, there is no doubt that as soon as he endures the suffering of a counter-evil, he will himself immediately want to exert a counter-counter-evil against his accuser, and thereby designate himself at once as guilty. In both cases, the counter-evil makes or reinforces the guilt of the guilty one, who it accuses and appoints. But there is more: not only can (must!) everyone become guilty, but the very movement by which I can recognize and provoke this guilt—the counter-evil—qualifies me as guilty, too, since I can quite legitimately exert it on anyone, because in exerting it I automatically render the accused guilty of it: I exert an unjust suffering on a possible innocent and do so in full justice. I become just as guilty as those I accuse, precisely because I do nothing but defend myself: it is in wanting to deliver myself from evil that I perpetuate it and universalize it. The logic of evil triumphs again, and always in the same manner: accuse them all, for evil will always find its own, since everyone in fact makes use of evil's unique logic. Revenge: a so-called innocent becomes, *justly,* an unjust culprit by transferring his suffering onto a presumed innocent, who, at once, in wanting to avenge himself, becomes a culprit in turn. The call for justice can only go forth by perpetuating iniquity—by justifying it.

In its logic, then, evil in no way forbids what we so often call the search for justice. Rather, it sets out to give the search for justice a rigorous conceptual status and the means to develop itself. Thus the worst thing about evil is perhaps not the suffering, nor even the innocent suffering, but rather that revenge appears to be its only remedy; the worst thing about evil is not, in a sense, the hurt, but the logic of revenge that triumphs even in the (apparent) reestablishment of justice, in the (temporary) cessation of suffering, in the (unstable) balance of injustices. For evil consists first in its transmission, which reproduces it without end by compensation, readjustment, reparation, in short by justice itself, without ever being able to stop. Doing evil would not come so naturally if it clearly and straightaway required a perverse intervention and a deliberate will—which, at least at the beginning, we do not have. However, an apparently legitimate intention's first reflex is enough: make the suffering I endure stop. For this simple intention leads to the accusation, then to the designation of an (innocent) culprit, finally to a counter-evil; the wholly natural intention attains its goal (to suppress a suffering) only by producing another moment of evil. Far from suspending and suppressing the evil, the natural intention compensates (or believes it compensates) for an evil with a counter-evil, which is to say that it perpetuates the evil. The height of evil consists in perpetuating evil with the intention of suppressing suffering, in rendering others guilty in order to guarantee one's own innocence. For the more I want to assure my innocence—as is quite natural!— the more I must discharge my sufferings and my responsibilities on someone else, in short the more I must engulf him in evil. "Am I my brother's keeper?" retorts Cain (and we with him) to God. The response, in remaining implicit, is expressed all the more clearly: "Of course not! If someone is my brother's keeper, it would be anyone other than me! If, of the two of us, one has to be responsible, it is my brother, who is responsible for my unhappiness by the simple fact that he remains happy when I no longer am."

To Endure Evil, or to Transmit It

This paradox opens onto another paradox, even more painful to hear. Without a doubt, the only way not to perpetuate evil would consist in not attempting to rid oneself of it *(s'en défaire)*, so as not to risk engulfing someone else in it. To keep one's suffering for oneself, rather than making a hypothetical culprit suffer it: to endure it, or as ordinary language puts it so well, to absorb the cost—as one can absorb a counterfeit bill. Indeed, suffering can be compared to a counterfeit bill: either one absorbs it and admits a total loss, inasmuch as it has no value and nothing will compensate its possessor; or one attempts to pass it off, that is to say, attempts to recuperate the good the counterfeiter has stolen by in turn robbing any new victim available; but in this case, I can "fix" my loss only if I put "the fix" on someone else and can assure equity for myself only by bringing about iniquity for someone other than me. "The truth of this world is death. You have to choose: death or lies."[4] Consisting first of all in its transmission, evil can be vanquished only by breaking this transmission, that is, by blocking it (as a player blocks a ball, bearing its shock). Several consequences follow. Christ vanquishes evil only by refusing to transmit it, enduring it to the point of running the risk, in "blocking" it, of dying; the just man is precisely he who endures evil without rendering it, suffers without claiming the right to make others suffer, suffers as if he were guilty. Next: he who claims to excuse himself absolutely, and thus refuses to endure evil without immediately transmitting it, can acquit himself only by accusing others; and in fact, original sin intervenes according to a schema of self-justifications accusative of the other: to God who asks for the sinner, Adam responds that he has no responsibility whatsoever—and transmits the responsibility to Eve, who, in turn, transmits it to the serpent; sin enters the world replete with the entire logic of evil: transmit evil to the other so as to rid one's self of it and in this way lay claim to innocence. Sin cannot be separated from the logic of its transmission.

---

[4] Louis-Ferdinand Céline, *Voyage au bout de la nuit,* in *Romans* vol. 1, ed. H. Godard (Paris: Pléiade, 1981), p. 200; *Journey to the End of the Night,* tr. Ralph Manheim (New York: New Directions, 1983), p. 173. One thinks here of Robert Bresson's admirable fable *L'Argent,* where evil's entire ignoble and crucial scope is produced through a single trivial, paltry, run of the mill counterfeit bill, the transmission of which never ceases to do evil.

From which there is a final consequence: he who contests the doctrine of original sin, by arguing that he bears no responsibility for original sin, repeats, from the very fact of this argument, all the logic of evil (self-justification, refusal to take evil upon oneself so as to block its transmission, and so forth), and thus inscribes himself completely in that very sinfulness of which he claims to know nothing; to declare oneself innocent of original sin and of its transmission, amounts, ineluctably and immediately, to repeating in an originary way, for one's own account, its fulfillment, and therefore to confirming its all-powerful logic. As for claims to the right to accuse God, because He is the cause of evil—an argument as banal as it is apparently powerful—this may very well constitute the supreme stage of the logic of revenge: the last culprit whom one who endures a universal evil can accuse is God. The ultimate service that God can render a humanity preyed upon by the spirit of revenge would thus be to furnish it with an even better culprit, the very best culprit indeed, since He lends Himself admirably and silently to an accusation exasperated by universal evil; in order that I, indeed that we all may be innocent of every evil that passes through us, it suffices for us to avenge ourselves of this evil on He who will not avenge Himself, to transmit the counter-evil to an absolute and universal neighbor. But who, in the infernal circle of this world, could bear and even conceive the simple thought that "the iniquity of us all lays upon him" without "opening his mouth, like a lamb that is led to the slaughter, like a sheep that before its shearers is dumb and opens not its mouth" (Isaiah 53:6–7)? No one among us, evidently: we would all be incapable of refraining from "proclaiming our innocence," that is to say, from avenging ourselves by defending ourselves. The neighbor who is universally and silently guilty, without defense or rejoinder, evil without counter-evil, thus does not belong to this world— God alone will furnish him to the world. Which is not possible, except at only one price: that, effectively, he be absolutely guilty, and thus, absolutely punished, and thus, absolutely dead. The "death of God" descends in this manner from the spirit of revenge, in a direct line. For the world, the only good God is a dead God. In as much as a living God appears odious to the world, so much does he, dead, become almost bearable, in order to satisfy the hate exerted by revenge. The world recognizes God only in order to be able to kill him—and God renders the world even this ultimate service.

In this way, evil deploys its logic as a logic of revenge, which gathers strength from the fact that man, spontaneously, finds in it the most evident recourse against the injustice of suffering. Iniquity deepens in proportion to our desire for justice, or rather our desire for *our* justice; the reciprocal guilt of all grows in just proportion to each one's declarations of innocence; evil transmits itself better to my neighbor the more I claim to be rid of it. In these paradoxical imbrications, which make a trap of iniquity, it becomes possible to intuit a mystery.

SUICIDE

Iniquity thus manifests, at least partially, its logic. It remains for us to attain its mystery, which would consist in nothing less than a "person," Satan. Yet, how would the deduction from logic to mystery not contradict itself, by claiming to pass from a reason to a folly, and, even more, to make of this folly an individual? However, even this apparently unthinkable transition can sketch an argumentation that supports it. Evil, then, deploys revenge as its only logic. Revenge can, like a flood engulfing the universe, reach every man, make of all humanity, and even of God, a culprit and an adversary. The world will stop furnishing defendants well before revenge ceases finding culprits in it. Thus, revenge passes beyond all limits, beginning with those of reality: it is thus practiced against the dead, whose physical disappearance in no way results in a nonsuit but, rather, exacerbates their guilt all the more: easy prey, these dead can neither defend themselves, nor, as vanished victims, atone. Whence the phantasmal exercise of revenge within a past that it unceasingly reconstructs according to its needs (as ideology remakes, or "fixes," history). Such an overflowing—in the strict sense—of revenge beyond reality indicates that, left to its logic, revenge prefers anything to no longer avenging itself. Which imposes an obligatory consequence: *better to avenge myself on myself than to cease avenging myself.* The triumph of revenge consists in turning against itself. This is not about nihilism, which turns the will out onto nothingness in order to preserve it there—better to want nothing than not to want at all—but about suicide, in which revenge is only preserved by turning itself against its own agent, which of course implies destroying him. Let us refrain from seeing in this a pure and simple contradiction; or rather, such a contradiction seems perfectly fitting here because, from its first stage on, revenge contradicts (accuses, destroys). That it therefore contradicts even the ontic support of its exercise certainly pushes the contradiction to its maximum; but, as contradiction constitutes its very essence, the maximum of its contradiction brings revenge to its final blossoming: suicide. "I am the wound, and the rapier! / I am the cheek, I am the slap! / I am the limbs, I am the rack, / The prisoner, the torturer! / I am my own blood's epicure."[5] Suicide, the terminal figure of the logic of evil, makes manifest its rigorous design; it reveals therefore its original and normative structure; in this way, every suicide remains a widely scaled act of revenge; when I accuse and kill the other (even when he is truly guilty), I bar myself from every reconciliation with him, thus depriving myself of what, deep down, I wish for above all else—not only to make my suffering cease, but also, more than to suppress its cause, to transform the cause of evil into a cause of happiness: suppressing the cause of my suffering implies therefore that I have already renounced try-

---

[5] Charles Baudelaire, *Les Fleurs du Mal,* "L'héautontimorouménos," in *Oeuvres Complètes,* éd. Y.-G. Le Dantec (Paris: Pléiade, 1961), p. 74; *The Flowers of Evil,* tr. James McGowan (New York: Oxford University Press, 1993), p. 157.

ing to make it useful, or trying to transform it; in short, trying to commune with it. By killing Desdemona, Othello believes he is suppressing the cause of his present suffering, but, obscurely, he knows that he is also suppressing the cause (possible in the future, just as it was real formerly) of a happiness to reestablish: to kill out of pure and simple revenge is already to deprive oneself of a reconciliation, and therefore of love: revenge does not reestablish the prior state, but condemns the future to an irremediable impossibility of loving; it does not restore to the present its past plenitude, but wrecks the possibility by insulting the future. Whence the absurd but lucid avowal of Othello as he stands before the sleeping beauty of Desdemona: "Be thus when thou art dead, and I will kill thee, / And love thee after."[6] Othello's suicide follows the murder of Desdemona because, for Othello, killing seems only to conclude the logic of revenge; in fact, however, killing directs it. Thus it is that every institutional form of revenge deploys a suicidal conduct, even and above all if it never finishes doing away with itself. Who has not seen this in the political arena? The more a political power perverts its exercise of power into an infinite revenge, the more it must finish by avenging itself on itself: the tyrant is diffident, the political police are overseen by still other police, the party purges itself regularly, the *praesidium*, finally, is peopled only by old men who continue living solely on the condition of having, for a long time, killed in themselves that which makes a man alive—the soul, or whatever one wants to call it. Without a doubt, the revolution persists in claiming that it works for happiness; but, like Othello, it is after the death of everyone that it will finally be able to begin to love. Evil loves us, but only after having brought us to death.

---

[6] William Shakespeare, *The Tragedy of Othello*, V, ii, 18–9. Likewise the emblematic maxim of "the madman of Shanghai": *"je vais d'abord vous couper la tête. Ensuite vous connaîtrez la verité!"* (First I'll cut off your head. Then you'll know the truth!) (Hergé, *Le lotus bleu*, 1946/1947 edition, p. 13; note, however, a variant: *"et vous connaîtrez alors la verité"* (and thus you shall know the truth), 1932 edition, p. 26; reprinted in *Archives Hergé* vol. 3, [Tournai: Casterman, 1979], p. 167).

THE ULTIMATE EVIL

To commit suicide, or more simply to kill oneself, amounts to making the logic of revenge triumph in oneself. Consequently, a suicide can last a lifetime; he who hates himself can never have enough life left in which to accuse himself, knowing as he does how to find within himself motives and pretexts for infinite (self) implication. Moreover, in waiting to finish himself off, the living suicide, playing the logic of evil to the hilt, experiences the ecstatic pleasure of an inverted *cogito*: I hate myself, therefore I am; and doubly, since, if I am, as accused (summoned to appear, and thus named! recognized guilty, thus recognized!), I am also the all-powerful accuser. As with revenge, the suicide that brings it to its ultimate achievement offers pleasures, which, insofar as they offer absolutely no joy, are all the more seductive. The worst is always true; the proof: I can always accomplish it, provided that I limit myself to my own territory; I can always avenge myself, and thus exert mastery, provided that I exert it on and against what always returns to me as my share, irremediably imparted to me—myself. Suicide thus offers to egoism its masterpiece: revenge that is absolute and always possible, the affirmation of self by the negation of self, which depends on nothing but self reduced to nothing. Which means that in committing suicide, I find myself in the same position— exactly—as if I avenged myself against the entire world: I am its master. And this is precisely why we all experience suicide as a temptation: the temptation not of nothingness but, through mastery of nothingness, of absolute mastery; literally, I commit suicide in order to avenge myself on the world. We must not dismiss too quickly the Faustian myth as a romantic masquerade, for Faust chose to lose his soul in order to master the world, which means: to commit suicide (in terms of the absolute) in order to avenge himself (a whole biological life long); his suicide admits only the time span of a mortal, the time to enjoy revenge. He masters the lives of others only on the condition of having already lost his own; he therefore exerts the authority of death, and, far from triumphing over death, he triumphs only through death. Faust sins through and against the spirit, whereas Don Giovanni still hesitates, caught by the flesh of desire, between life and death. Faust enjoys revenge, while Don Giovanni suffers revenge, because he still enjoys. Only the spirit can really kill itself, because it alone is pure—and therefore powerful enough to deny (itself). In this way, evil rightly promises us "to be as gods" in the absolute independence that renders me master of myself and of the universe. Suicide must therefore be understood fundamentally as a sin, indeed as *the* sin: that of mimicking God by absenting oneself from creation's logic of love, in and through a de-creation's logic of revenge. To prefer to master absolutely, though it come at the price of killing oneself, over receiving, though it be the grace to become a son of God; to prefer the nothing that I produce to the infinite gift that I receive. Every sin, at bottom, comes from the logic of revenge and leads to what founds it, namely suicide. Within every logic of revenge, evil triumphs in suicide, its ultimate figure.

DECEPTION

But, one might object, what can be more honest than this alternative? How can we speak of "iniquity," since human freedom has never before found itself placed before a more just and more complete alternative? Before such a logic, how could we suppose the least "mystery," in that a logic whose constraining rigor our entire analysis wanted to underline summons the freedom of man, in full knowledge of the cause (revenge)? How, above all, should we, so as to give an account of this hypothetical "mystery of iniquity," make an appeal, as slight as it might be, to an authority other than human freedom, to the point of joining to this mystery an other freedom and giving this other freedom the name of a person? Before turning to this third question, we must first comply with the first two and examine their common presupposition: that the logic of revenge, in leading to suicide,

offers not an iniquitous but a rational option. Now, on the
contrary, it seems possible to show that the logic of revenge
is achieved in and on the other side of suicide (referring to
the suicide that lasts a lifetime), by a deception, or better by
several deceptions. The first deception is glimpsed as early as
the formulation of the essence of suicide (as the completion
of revenge): I would not commit suicide if I did not hope to
gain thereby, paradoxical but all the more real: revenge, and
therefore mastery. Nothingness is desired certainly for itself,
but, as it immediately implies revenge, and revenge implies
mastery, and as mastery seems to me—even emptied of all
reality—to constitute my own affirmation, I desire my sui*cide*
because thereby I hope for my *sui*cide, thus a good—myself.
Evil, wanted for itself, becomes, for that very reason, my
final good, my self's final word. But, in reality, what does
the suicide actually receive? The question is not at all point-
less, once we admit that suicide completes revenge, inasmuch as it begins with the first exercise of revenge, well
before culminating in physical killing; and what is more, we
know revenge from experience. So, then, what does revenge
give to anyone who entrusts himself to it? Quite exactly
nothing. Nothing means first of all: no real good, for the
more possession increases, the more it becomes null and indifferent; absolute possession possesses nothing but itself; if
we think the contrary, without a doubt it is because we do
not possess enough to know that possession deprives us of
the very thing we possess—because in possessing it, we no
longer meet in it any other reality besides our own consumption of it, that is to say, we meet ourselves, alone.[7] But
nothing also means: no communion with anyone; if revenge
kills (me), it does not allow a reign (as the promise of mastery

---

[7] See the startling description of the nothingness possessed within a dia-
bolically dominated world, as painted by Balzac in *Melmoth réconcilié*. What
the "pact with the devil" gains for man is everything, thus everything possessed, thus nothing. As Midas dies from transmuting what he touches into
gold, the rich man asphyxiates himself by transforming into himself—into
his multiple idol—what he appropriates as his own/for himself. The self-
possessed man possesses only himself; and so he's done for!

has assured) except over the dead; to reign over the dead amounts to not reigning at all; for self-affirmation, even through suicide, aims always for recognition—precisely because it mimics it perversely by inverting it—and thus for communion; whoever avenges himself seeks in the gaze of whoever he accuses and punishes the recognition of his own justice; the more he avenges himself, the more he demands that someone recognize his justice. But in order to avenge himself, he must also kill the witness; he must close the very eyes from which he nevertheless demands a justificatory look. The suicide pushes this paradox to infinity: he kills the last culprit, but also the last witness; and perhaps suicide would tempt us less if we came to it after having sufficiently practiced revenge, that is to say, killed enough nevertheless indispensable witnesses so that, in killing ourselves, we indeed killed, along with the last culprit, the last witness of our justice. We commit suicide poorly, having not killed all men—this fact thus conceals from us suicide's first deceit: that it removes from the triumph of revenge even the means of tasting it. The logic of evil promises us mastery in and through nothingness, therefore a perfect justification before the world and ourselves; but the price of nothingness becomes, in the moment of suicide, infinite—nothingness, in consequence, takes hold of the possessor of himself, of the master of nothingness; nothingness permits me to win myself only be annihilating myself; the victory of nothingness indeed annihilates the universe, but it also abolishes the witness and the beneficiary of the annihilating revenge (me). Suicide (as the truth of revenge) does not only suppress, along with life, the reasons to live; it kills, with life, the very reasons for killing oneself. Revenge, in one fell swoop, breaks the treaty and the barrier: it submerges even the avenger, who loses control of it in the very moment of gathering its fruit—or rather, not in the very moment, but just before. Just before—there's the horror! Iniquity appears immediately: I believe, in avenging myself, that I am winning my justification; in fact, however, I am eliminating the conditions for its recognition; I believe, by committing suicide, that I am win-

ning everything through nothing; in fact, I am losing
everything for nothing—for nothingness *(pour le rien).* Iniquity, as dupery of the avenger by the logic of evil, robs me
of my very suicide. I thus lose even the nothing to which I
sacrificed everything.

Hell Imprisons Me, Hell Lies to Me
(L'enfermement—L'enfer me ment)

To notice this dupery and to measure its irreducibility as well
as its amplitude is sufficient perhaps to constitute what is
named Hell, and to busy the soul with it. As soon as revenge
is accomplished against myself or against another, I comprehend that, far from having rectified the relation to the other,
I have destroyed the very possibility of even the least relation, distorted or justified, between him and me. Thus the
logic of evil does not, in the end, grant me what it had
promised. Instead of suppressing unjust suffering, it sup-
presses the conditions of every relation, and therefore of all
justice—whence the iniquity of the logic of evil. For the first
time, the logic of evil turns against the one who put it into
operation. In suicide, this logic did not turn against him, but
only applied itself to him in order better to serve his intention to carry out revenge—or at least so it claimed. Here, on
the contrary, the logic of evil turns against whoever uses it,
because it betrays him: the user discovers himself used. Evil
betrays: whoever appeals to the logic of evil in order to
avenge himself always believes that he is relying on a power,
a knowledge, in short, on an authority other than himself; in
noticing that evil has a logic, he believes that he knows evil;
in a word, he "believes" in it, puts his confidence in it as in
a verified theory, an efficient and just practice, a pure and
simple means of attaining his goals. But the betrayal breaks
out from the very moment evil actually puts its logic into
operation: the logic of evil is not a means, it is an end; therefore, it destroys a culprit (revenge) only by forbidding every
relation (even justified) with others, or with oneself; conse-

quently, it kills indifferently the "enemy" and the "friend," precisely because it recognizes only "enemies." The logic of evil betrays whoever puts the least confidence in it. Such is Hell—probably: comprehending this betrayal; or rather, comprehending in this betrayal that Hell is the absence of every other.[8] And doubly so. Through suicide (as the completion of revenge), the logic of evil destroys, with the adversary, the very possibility of every future relation, therefore all future justice: revenge as the amputation of the possible. What is more, suicide destroys in me the possibility and the dignity of being a witness to a possible relation; in short, it abolishes the gap within the person (distance) that, in advance, fits him to the very possibility of a communion. After suicide (revenge), the other is excluded from the possible world: every other becomes impossible because the logic of evil has destroyed in me the space of alterity (distance). Hell is therefore the moment when the soul finds itself finally alone, or, as we say with naive longing, "unified": a widow of distance, alone not only because isolated but above all because constitutively powerless to sustain the separation from oneself that alone renders possible the welcoming of another as other. In this way the soul discovers itself to be alone only insofar as it voluntarily becomes a solitude. Hell imprisons (L'enfer enferme): it closes the soul in on itself, by means of an imprisonment which, to close itself ever more narrowly, never ceases to shrink the promised mastery over the world unto nothing, or rather to reduce the world in which this sovereign control is exerted unto nothing. Hell imprisons the soul in itself.[9] But the absence of any other results even more directly from the betrayal: for betrayal itself consists in

---

[8] The slogan "Hell is other people" (L'enfer c'est les autres) reveals such a crude misinterpretation that, apart from a simple trademark expression thrown out to the general public, one must read in it either the admission of complete ignorance of both other people and of Hell, or a supreme lie of the sort that evil utters in order to disguise its logic. You choose.

[9] Here again, we will take Balzac seriously: in La peau de chagrin, the world is given to be possessed and mastered only on condition that the soul ascertains with its own eyes the shrinking of its true world (the temporal delay transposing the spatial and spiritual shrinking).

the desertion of the other. Indeed, to the one who avenges and/or kills himself, the logic of evil seems to propose itself as a power, a knowledge, in short as an authority other than himself, in which he can "believe." But, the logic of evil betrays this confidence by giving mastery only over nothing, by imprisoning *(enfermant)* the soul in the Hell *(l'enfer)* of this nothing. And the soul, thus imprisoned, cannot appeal a decision that it alone made: here the trap shows itself; the soul believes that it is committing itself to a reality other than itself—the very logic of evil—but, once it has committed suicide in total "confidence," it discovers not only that it has lost everything and itself, but above all that it cannot appeal this forfeiture—because there is nobody to appeal it to. *Hell lies to me (L'enfer me ment).* The betrayal culminates in the absence of the betrayer: the soul was deceived by the logic of evil, but the logic of evil traps it yet again, in that a logic never speaks, nor can it ever respond, as a responsible party: the soul had only to comprehend this logic correctly and the betrayal would do nothing but reflect existentially a lack of theoretical intelligence; the soul was indeed deceived, but it was always the soul that deceived itself: not only was it swindled out of its mastery and imprisoned in an internal Hell, but it is further swindled out of a responsible party, as well. Hell betrays, and, to cap it off, leases out the role of betrayer to the very one who finds himself betrayed. The logic of revenge, which always discovers some responsible party, even in the victim (suicide), only refuses to subpoena one responsible party—itself: it sidesteps its own responsibility and renders accountable for its own betrayal the soul that it betrays. For a second time, it betrays the one who it betrayed (in deceiving him) by its refusal to admit its treachery. Hell is the absence of every other: betrayal flees its responsibility, the betrayer betrays by stealing away from the triumph of his betrayal. The soul discovers itself alone for a second time: abandoned by the very one who abandons it, the soul can only—as everyday language puts it—take it out on itself. That is to say, kill itself a second time (the "second death"), with an endless suicide.

THE MISSING BETRAYER

But don't we now have the best proof, and so to speak a priori, that Satan does not exist, because Hell consists only in a betrayal without betrayer? The disappearance of all recourse to some other—to some sort of accountable party—is reinforced by a final success: if the soul cannot accuse anyone of being responsible (except itself), this is because, to begin with, it *was not* even deceived. For, in fact, like Macbeth, the soul literally was not deceived: the logic of revenge had, in fact, announced the destruction of the other and a mastery limited to ruling over nothingness. Macbeth did not take seriously the prophecies that he would remain unvanquished only as long as Birnam Wood does not come to Dunsinane Hill, and that he would not be killed by "one of woman born"; he saw in these announcements only a metaphor for unexpected invulnerability—by which he showed the pathological naivete of those who want to be realistic at any cost. Once the two announcements are fulfilled in the event, Macbeth, before he dies, becomes indignant: "be these juggling fiends no more believed, / That palter with us in a double sense, / That keep the word of promise to our ear, / And break it to our hope" (V, vii, 19–22). Macbeth is wrong to exclaim so: the witches did not lie to him, for their predictions, far from deceiving, were verified literally; it was his blindness alone, resulting from the false evidence of a self-serving interpretation, that deceived him. The soul, like Macbeth, did not want to hear what the logic of revenge was actually proposing; the destruction of the other (accusation and universal guilt) signified what it signifies—the disappearance of every other, without exception, including myself as the very condition of alterity (distance)—and not a simple elimination of enemies; the mastery of nothingness signified what it signifies, literally that mastery is exercised over nothing, over nothingness *(le rien)*. For evil at least respects its logic—that of the letter without the spirit. Evil remains literal, it literally does evil to the letter. Mephistopheles wants a contract from Faust, not a spoken promise but a letter, for lying lies to the letter, innocently. The soul therefore was not deceived, it deceived itself. It has no option left but to take it out on itself, "only to expose profanely / Eternal absence" of itself, the betrayer who betrays his word only by respecting it to the letter, and who sidesteps his responsibility only inasmuch as he holds responsibility by not holding it.[10] Henceforth, then, must we not conclude that the betrayal without betrayer and the promise kept by logic deploy evil to the point of the second suicide precisely without requiring any agent outside the very logic of revenge? We would thus be exempted from introducing the "person" of Satan. But our analysis in fact results in the exact inverse. Or better, it flushed out Satan only a moment ago. For Satan reveals himself precisely in the way in which he sidesteps responsibility—and thereby perfectly accomplishes the logic of evil: "Ah, how alone we are in evil, my brother! [. . .] From now until the end of the world, the sinner will always have to sin alone, always alone—for just as we die alone, so also do we sin alone. The devil, you see, is that friend who never stays with us till the end."[11] Satan, a *satan*, indicates, in Hebrew, an "accuser" (Job 1:6; Zachariah 3:1; and so on) who wants the death of man to come about through lies that in all sincerity "he speaks according to his own nature" (John 8:44). Indeed, all these characteristics have already found their place in the outline of a deduction that we have just conducted: Satan accuses men, apparently for the benefit of one among them, in fact in order that this very one might end up accusing himself and putting himself to death without end or respite; but the trap thus laid can function in all its perfection only if the last man can no longer extricate

---

[10] Stéphane Mallarmé, *"Une dentelle s'abolit / Dans le doute du Jeu suprème / A n'entr'ouvrir comme un blasphème / Qu'absence éternelle de lit"* (*Oeuvres Complètes* [Paris: Pléiade, 1945], p. 74). "Lace sweeps itself aside / In the doubt of the ultimate Game / Only to expose profanely / eternal absence of bed" (Mallarmé, *Collected Poems*, tr. Henry Weinfield [Berkeley: University of California Press, 1994], p. 80).

[11] Georges Bernanos, *Monsieur Ouine* (*Oeuvres Romanesques* [Paris: Pléiade, 1963], p. 1490); *Monsieur Ouine,* tr. William S. Bush (Lincoln: University of Nebraska Press, 2000), p. 171.

himself *(se défaire)* from his responsibility (with regard to his
victims, but also with regard to his own self) except by accusing himself; in order to do this, Satan must disappear—
betray confidence, and betray his own betrayal by stealing
away. Only this stealing away closes Hell shut: Hell is the absence of every other, *even of Satan*; the trap becomes infernal
only if its victim finds himself definitively imprisoned there,
and thus solely responsible.[12] It is said that Satan's strength
consists in making us believe that he does not exist. We must
deepen this trivialized paradox. It means that Satan dissimulates himself, first of all, in the logic of evil, in order better
to make us believe his quasi-innocence; but above all it
means that, once the logic of evil is irremediably put into
motion toward the ultimate disaster, Satan must steal away
so that the soul can no longer rid itself *(se défaire)* of its death
by putting it onto someone else, and, betrayed by a betrayal
without betrayer, continually undo itself *(se défaire)* without
end—Sisyphus of its own defeat. More than a ruse, the absence of Satan constitutes his sole mode of action. He thus
mimics God, whose retreat provides for the distance in
which only sons and daughters may be created and adopted;
but the mimicry—Satan the ape of God—veers toward caricature, for distance constitutes a mode of God's pressing love
and thus makes man live, whereas Satan's slipping away provokes the soul to kill itself out of a nameless hatred. Satan
tempts, deceives, and kills insofar as he dissimulates and slips
away. His ungraspable flight, far from reducing him to a fac-
ultative hypothesis, flushes him out as a presupposition
whose groundwork is operative only insofar as it slips away.
Satan slips away *(se dérobe)* (a betrayer fleeing responsibility
for the betrayal) only as ground slips away under the feet as
soon as one's step seeks to press upon the soil. In slipping
away, Satan adds to revenge as the logic of evil by manifest-
ing its intention and its essence—evasion *(dérobade)* itself.
Revenge cultivates only an evasion, and aims only to rob

---

[12] This is the masterful demonstration of the work of Edgar-Pierre Ja-
cobs, *Le piège diabolique* (Neuilly-sur-Seine: Dargaud, 1962).

man of his soul, which simply reveals the final evasion that is Satan, in person.

The Absolute Idiot

But one must understand that, if Satan is and acts only by evasion, this is for him less a ruse than a necessity: he can do neither better nor otherwise. If he does not confront man openly, perhaps this is first of all because he does not have the means to dare to do so. A fundamental reason forbids him this audacity: he himself is situated in Hell; even better, he constitutes a hell par excellence, as the closed site where access to every other is definitively shut off; Satan, by abolishing the filial distance within himself, is forbidden constitutively from inhabiting the distance in which God gives himself, and in which the (adoptive) sons and daughters of the Father give themselves to one another in the Son. If we can never encounter Satan, so as to record his existence, the impossibility no doubt comes from the unsurpassable imprisonment of Satan, orphan of distance, decidedly unsuited to bear alterity as such. Faced with an adoptive son whom the Father adopts, faced with Christic distance, Satan can attempt/tempt nothing *(Satan ne peut rien tenter)* because he experiences his powerlessness in the face of distance. This is indeed why exorcism reaches him, throwing into his disfigured face his powerlessness to distance by invoking the name before which every knee bends, in heaven, on earth, and in Hell (Philippians 2:10). We must give up imagining Satan as all-powerful: he is capable of nothing, or more exactly, only of what can become nothing, through possession; he is capable of nothing to counter the filial distance he has lost. Properly speaking, Satan is an undone son *(un fils défait)*, undone of his filiation, who experiences the filiation of men as a defeat *(défaite)*, for which he must avenge himself, by undoing *(défaisant)* it. We must give up definitively a false alternative concerning Satan, on one hand denying him too much (even his very existence), or on the other according him too much (an omnipotent existence); both the one and the other hypothesis effectively miss the crucial point: that Satan prospers only from a diminished existence, a defeated personality, strictly a personality that has become impersonal through the loss of filial distance. Satan's power remains, angelic certainly, and therefore incommensurable with ours, and spreads over thoughts as over things, over the spirit as over the world; but it stays permanently illiterate in charity, because decidedly deprived of distance. Satan can indeed call himself omnipotent, but, for all that, he remains no less impotent for love; he exerts his regional omnipotence only in order to render every man impotent to love—as by that cold and frenetic jealousy that novelists have attributed to eunuchs. Just as he exerts his omnipotence everywhere, in the order of the grandeurs of the flesh and that of the grandeurs of the spirit, so too, in the third order, "the least movement of charity" leaves him impotent. Whence his sudden cowardice, as stupefying as his former arrogance. If we must give to the imagination a sensible representation of Satan who steals away in order to steal us from ourselves, it would be just as well to prefer the one ventured by Dante: "The emperor of the dolorous kingdom," frozen in the ice, from which, like Mallarmé's swan, he cannot shake the "white agony," "was as beautiful then as he now is ugly": the splendor of an icon of God is, in him, monstrously transformed into its opposite, bestiality; the three pairs of wings of the seraphim remain, "but their mode was like a bat's"; by his three faces, he vaguely imitates the Trinity, in inverting it: the first face, red, betrays hatred, the second, white and yellow, marks envious impotence, the last, black, ignorance. Satan cries and slobbers at no longer being able to inhabit distance, that is to say at no longer being a person.[13] Prince

---

[13] Dante Alighieri, *Inferno,* XXXIV, v. 28, 34, 49, 37–45, 53–54; see the excellent findings of A. Valensin, "Le diable dans la divine comédie," in *Satan* (Paris: Les Etudes Carmélitaines, 1948), which concludes: "Lucifer is nothing more—we must pair these two terms—than a *bestial thing*" (531), in the sense perhaps in which Yves Bonnefoy speaks of an "old cerebral bestiary" (*Du mouvement et de l'immobilité de Douve* [Paris: Mercure de France, 1953], p. 25), and in which, for Bernanos, Ouine "no longer

of the sorrowful kingdom, of the hell that shuts out the soul from distance, thus stealing its humanity by forbidding it to commune with God, he alienates himself by forbidding himself alterity; therefore, he can only (as in an inverted and transposed onto-theology) concentrate onto himself all its horror: he can steal away from all those whom he thus imprisons in hell, and from everything, but he cannot avoid the imprisonment itself of hell: "but not the horror of the earth where the plumage is caught" (Mallarmé, "Le vierge, le vivace et le bel aujourd'hui"). More than every other soul, Satan suffers from hell, the ultimate circle of which binds him in a solitude so absolute, an identity so perfect, a consciousness so lucid and a sincerity so transparent to itself, that he becomes there the absolute negative of the person—the perfect idiot. Satan, or the perfect idiot: *ídios,* the one who assumes his particularity as a proper good, who appropriates his own identity to such a point that he first does not want and then is not able to "leave himself," that is to say, to inhabit distance. Madness, in its most thoroughly accomplished human forms, offers only a distant outline of the absolute idiocy of Satan, in whom lucidity, powerlessness, self-hatred, and envy combine to engender a suffering whose very paroxysm becomes so unbearable that it obliges the person to fade into a state of insensibility in which life mimics death at its closest. In order to trigger endlessly and aimlessly the imprisonment of a treachery traitor to itself, Satan swallows himself up ceaselessly and without rest in the idiocy of his own expropriation—a black hole of the soul, which gradually absorbs the soul into its very absence. "I am empty, too."[14] Absolute idiot, enclosure from distance, personality empty of any living person: Satan does not let us prove his existence easily, for in fact his existence is as good as wholly

---

had any human meaning," and, dead, showed himself reduced to "a life henceforth without cause or goal, like that of a little maleficent beast" (*Monsieur Ouine,* pp. 1560, 1562; tr. Bush, pp. 254, 256, translation modified).

[14] Confession of Ouine, according to Bernanos, p. 1550; tr. Bush, p. 243.

annihilated. Satan, or the almost total defeat of the person. Almost? There still remains the trace of what he effaces, enough of the personal so that—when his evasion hides behind "nobody" *(personne)*[15]—we might know what he kills in us after having killed it in himself: the icon of the invisible. Almost? There is still God's part.

THE PERSON AND THE WILL

But how to explain now that what barely even exists can nonetheless threaten us and come to meet us? Must we object to the previous analysis, or suspect the testimony of the spiritual authors? Neither one. If Satan is summed up in a defeat of the person, if he also attempts to accuse man in order to kill the humanity in him (that is to say, the *similitudo Dei*), the only end that can still stir him will therefore be to put to death the person in man. Only this destruction can mobilize Satan: for Satan only acts and is as a *satan*, a public accuser who lives only "in session." Camus's Caligula confesses: "How strange! When I don't kill, I feel alone."[16] Satan for his part kills in order to reinforce the idiocracy *(l'idiotisme)*[17] of his solitude; or more exactly, he kills by rendering man as solitary as he is himself—by rendering man as much of an idiot as is he himself. In tempting man, that is to say in attempting to destroy the person in man, which upholds him as the likeness of God, Satan does not leave his idiocracy; on the contrary, he strengthens it by destroying any distance that would uphold the person in man. Satan destroys the person around him in order to protect himself from the person, and strengthens his idiocy with a nation of idiots, in his likeness

---

[15] [Translator's note: In French, *personne* without the article signifies "nobody," while *la personne* signifies "person." Both meanings are to be felt in the description throughout this essay of Satan's personhood.]

[16] Camus, *Caligula,* p. 102; tr. Gilbert, p. 68.

[17] [Translator's note: here and elsewhere in this book, the French word *l'idiotisme* (meaning not "idiom," as it usually does in French, but "extreme solitude, self-ownership") is translated by the English word "idiocracy": "personal rule or government" *(OED).*]

(and not in that of God), just as certain political regimes sur-
round themselves with satellite states, their mimes, victims,
and defenders. Thus, in inflicting temptation, Satan tries to
disfigure the person in man, to fill the distance within him,
to erase his *similitudo Dei*; temptation consists in the confrontation between a negative personality, negative because already murderous of his own person, and a person who
doubts his own personality: in temptation, a person fights to
empty a personality of his person. "When the words are
from the devil, not only do they fail to have good effects but
they leave bad ones. [. . .] I wonder if one spirit doesn't feel
the presence of the other spirit."[10] Satan searches for us, as a
hoodlum "searches out" a client in a gambling den, in order
to have a pretext for roughing him up and ripping him off;
ripping him off of what is important in him: money, or, for
Satan, the root of the person—that which can unite him to
God in Christ, the will. A personality empty because undone
(défaite) of his own person, Satan attempts to undo us *(nous
défaire)* of what makes us persons: free will. He imposes himself upon us only by the exemplary hyperbole of his own undoing, exerts his power only by virtue of an impotent
powerlessness of which we have no idea: he forces us to
nothingness by the inverted negative entropy of an unheard-
of humanity. His impotent powerlessness to will to love
loves only one thing: to will the impotent powerlessness of
our will so as to reassure his own impotent powerlessness.
Whence comes the ultimately rather banal game that we
know all too well: convincing us of our human and spiritual
nullity, highlighting our past failures in order to draw a fore-
cast of the future; repeating over and over to us that love is
impossible and that, in any event, we are incapable, unworthy, or frustrated—so it was with Judas, victim par excellence
of Satan: "He acted with enormous humility, he believed
himself unworthy of being good. [. . .] He thought that

---

[18] St. Teresa of Avila, *The Book of Her Life*, XXV, in *The Collected Works
of St. Teresa of Avila*, vol. 1, tr. Kieran Kavanaugh, O.C.D., and Otilio
Rodriguez, O.C.D. (Washington, D.C.: ICS Publications, 2d ed. 1987),
p. 217.

happiness, like good, is a divine attribute and not to be usurped by men."[19]

In this way, evil in person plunges us into a sadness so radical and dense that we despair of ever being able to escape it, that is to say of ever being able to *will* our escape from it. This sadness intends to resign us to suicide, but by our own account, through this sole will, the inanity of which it claims nonetheless to demonstrate. Satan does not have the means—the will—to modify or annihilate our will, since, in a sense, he has no more will: it remains for him to delude us into believing that we already have no more will (even though one remains in us) in order that, by ourselves, we willfully annihilate our will—suicide again. In temptation—the only one, that of despair, which all the others prepare and have in view—Satan appears to us as such: evil in person; but paradoxically: a personality empty of what makes the person (the free will to love), a personality who, in the mode of depersonalization, works indirectly to undo our person, so as to imprison us in the idiocy of hell. An abstract person: like Satan, we would thus caricature God.[20] Does Satan exist? But really, what does "to exist" mean here? Evil aims only to universalize what its reality—on the extreme fringe of nothingness—amounts to: a person bereft of all personality, an eternal absence inhabited only by this minimum of consciousness, which allows him to hate his inexistence; the person of Satan amounts to a nothingness that personalizes his despair. Like Ulysses escaping from the blinded Cyclops, Satan can indeed be called "nobody" *(personne)*: a person who hides only an absence of person; and thus the only indisputable proof of his "existence" comes to us from the

---

[19] Jorge Luis Borges, "Three Versions of Judas," in *Ficciones,* ed. Anthony Kerrigan (New York: Grove Press, 1962), p. 154.

[20] This is why Baudelaire's remark that "the devil . . . places great hope in imbeciles" (*Mon coeur mis à nu,* XVII, p. 1281), can be understood, outside its obvious meaning, with another specificity: Satan can place hope only in those who will let themselves weaken enough to become as weak as him, those who will be stupid enough to share his idiocracy; for Satan is weak, in the sense that Bernanos describes, "I too am empty, said M. Ouine," *Monsieur Ouine,* p. 1550; tr. Bush, p. 243.

abyss, the vertigo of which, often, pushes us to suicide. Van-
quishing Satan within us thus amounts simply to becoming
that which he can no longer achieve in himself—a person,
who, by himself, does not always will to avenge himself, or
at least wills not to avenge himself always. To will against the
logic of vengeance—what freedom would allow it?

March 1979

2

The Freedom to Be Free

In memory of Claude Bruaire

WHEN WE STAND before evil appearing in person but without personhood, our concern is with the will; we seek, without knowing exactly what we are talking about, to will as only what we call a person can will. To will as a person, or else to will to conduct oneself as a person, to take the role *(persona)* of a will willing irremediably, is sufficient to define an ethics. But ethics belongs, de facto and de jure, to metaphysics. Ever since Heraclitus wrote of *ethos* as the properly sacred dimension *(daimôn)*—ἦθος ἀνθρώπῳ δαίμων (fr. 199)—that which either determines or is lacking from the very humanity of man, what has always been at stake in ethics, for metaphysics, is man in his essential humanity. And this is why even Heidegger, when he attempts to think *ethos* more radically than metaphysical ethics had thought it, still aims only to avoid losing the humanity of man, or giving man up to *animalitas*. Every metaphysics, finally, completes itself in and can be judged by the ethics that it renders possible. But if modernity concludes metaphysics, what becomes of ethics? We venture to say here that, as a correlate to the end of metaphysics, modernity also witnesses the thorough undoing *(défaite)* of ethics. Let us be more precise: with the advent of modernity, ethics no longer finds itself contested in the application of its norms, nor in their definition (we no longer have disputes about the nature of the Sovereign Good, or about the actuality of a perfectly moral act); rather, its very foundations are contested. Modernity does not transgress the moral norm; it refuses the normality of the norm; in short, it transgresses transgression itself; it annuls the very law that justified the transgressiveness of transgression; it does not destroy ethics, it refuses it. Modernity refuses that ethics might ever impose upon it a norm coming absolutely from elsewhere, like the "Calm block here fallen from obscure disaster," whose granite Mallarmé wished would "at least mark the boundaries evermore / To the dark flights of Blasphemy hurled to the future."[1]

The transgression of transgression deploys itself on two fronts: (1) It contests the claim that certain norms may impose themselves on the conscience of an individual, that is to say, on a will; (2) It refuses the claim that any norm may impose itself on the conscience of an individual, that is to say, on a will. These two contestations proceed either politically or individually, in the name of either power or desire. We intend first to situate them metaphysically so as then to draw out their common presupposition.

Violence without Shadows

Let us take the following as the Kantian definition of the moral imperative by universality: "Act in such a manner that the maxim of your will can always be counted at the same time as the principal of a universal act of legislation." The motive for my action must be capable of becoming, without contradicting itself, the motive for the action of every other man; the test of universalization (assigning to others the maxim of my action) will either mark a contradiction (the absence of universality) or mark me with universality, and thus abstract me from everything within myself that belongs to the phenomenal (empirical particularity, pathology) and offends the rational. Abstraction is the price of universality: the moral good appears as an imperative because it deploys the abstraction of the noumena. Whence the Hegelian in-

---

[1] Stéphane Mallarmé, "Le Tombeau d'Edgar Poe," *Oeuvres Complètes* (Paris: Pléiade, 1945), p. 70; *Collected Poems,* tr. Henry Weinfield (Berkeley: University of California Press, 1994), p. 71.

junction to substitute a determined and concrete requirement for the universal and abstract norm. This is a
movement from morality, which makes demands, to the objective constraint of positive law, the universal abstracted to
the concrete necessities of the concept. However, this transition remains itself abstract, as long we do not consider it together with its corollary, not Hegelian but post-Hegelian:
ideology.[2] Hegel's attempt to determine the abstract moral imperative through the requirements of particularity and actuality made an appeal to the concept, as the tool of absolute
analysis. Hegel's historical descendants substituted for the
concept what can be called a "conception of the world."
Now, conceiving the world also implies producing it: producing a world, instead of speaking *this* world, splitting the
world into a real but unknown or ill-known world and a
world that is radically knowable precisely because produced
insofar as it is known—this is the function of ideology. Ideology produces a world that from the outset is in conformity
with the demands of discourse. Put another way, it claims to
offer reasons for what is by referring to what ought to be,
and it thus eventually authorizes destroying whatever is that
does not conform itself to what ought to be. Whereas the
(Hegelian) concept loses itself, as transparent rationality, in
the concrete, so as to reemerge, fertilized by the trial of the
negative, other and otherwise potent, (post-Hegelian) ideology prefers to lose the obscure actuality of the concrete,
eliminating it by violence if need be, in order to keep up the
illusory self-transparency of an empty discourse. And yet it is
no less true that ideology reinstalls, according to its own

---

[2] With, however, one exception: the mention of "what the French call
ideology" (G. W. F. Hegel, *Vorlesungen uber die Geschichte der philosophie,*
vol. 19, *Sämtliche Werke,* ed. H. Glockner [Stuttgart: Fr. Frommanns Verlag, 1965], pp. 505–506). But this example deals only with ideology in the
sense that Destutt de Tracy uses it. See E. Kennedy, " 'Ideology' from
Destutt de Tracy to Marx," *Journal of the History of Ideas* 40 (1979): 353–
368, and an early version of the present essay, "L'idéologie, ou la violence
sans ombre," *Revue catholique internationale Communio* V, no. 6 (1980):
82–92.

mode, the moral injunction: to the actuality of the world, it addresses an irresistible *du sollst!* This calls for two remarks:

(1) Here man no longer receives the injunction of rationality, which would require that in him the phenomenal be modified in such a way as to conform with the noumenal; on the contrary, rather, it is man who, as the master of rationality, enjoins reality to modify itself in accordance with the (supposedly) rational project. From whence it follows that the *du sollst!* addressed by man to the world can take an economic form just as well as a political form. The political form displays itself, par excellence, in Leninism and Nazism; in the two cases (more so in the first than in the second), an abstract model of society and finally of the entire world compels both to conform to it, no matter what the price. Force and terror intervene only afterwards, as means for implementing a requirement that claims to be theoretically, and thus rationally, justified. What makes the twentieth century a century of infernal reason (and, doubtless, not a century of barbarism[3]) is precisely the fact that violence, terror, and annihilation have for the first time claimed to be innocent, or, better, have claimed to be carrying out virtuously a painful moral task. In contrast, Macbeth knows the enormity of his crime—"I am afraid to think what I have done" (II.ii.49). Gnawed by remorse, he dies of not being able to render himself innocent of his crime. But no totalitarian master of our century has died of remorse, and neither will one die of not being able to justify himself rationally—for each has at his disposal a more or less elaborated, more or less impressive ideology ("socialism," war of liberation, national security, in decreasing order of efficacy), that suffices to render him innocent. Totalitarianism no longer undergoes the injunction of the

---

[3] Barbarism exerts its violence only against a rationality under siege, and thus against one recognized as such. In our time, a wholly other alliance has been formed: it is rationality itself that exerts violence and supports it. For it is no longer violence that stands up to discourse; instead, it can be—inversely—discourse that, as such, exerts a violence at least as great as that of physical force. Or, in the words of Alain Besançon, "to treat the Soviets as barbarians is unjust to the barbarians."

universal; rather, it exerts the injunction on the world. The universal moral imperative must yield the injunction to a particularism erected as absolute norm. Totalitarianism: to establish the concept of a supposed particular good as the only good that is rationally thinkable, and therefore morally justifiable. Whence the necessity of excluding whatever does not allow itself to be reduced in this way: destruction of that part of the actual people that refuses reduction (concentration camps, genocide), destruction of the thought that escapes it (intellectual and religious oppression), destruction of every world exterior to it (in actual terms, war; in imaginative terms, closing of borders; in terms of memory, falsification of records).

(2) Totalitarianism inverts the moral imperative: instead of judging itself, totalitarianism uses the moral imperative to judge the world. The act of correction is inverted: man does not correct his shortcomings by correcting what is particular in him through recourse to the universal; rather, he corrects the world by a rationality subjugated to his particular choices. But this schema supposes, first, that universal reason can reach the singular, and that it can then be mobilized by the initiative of a particularism. Up until now, we have been assuming a concept of ideology. Let us now assume a concept of technology. Why do we appeal to technology? Because it constitutes, par excellence, the form of rationality that, at the terminal point of metaphysics, submits beings in their totality to man as their master and possessor. How? By substituting another world for the world such as it is. This substitution clearly assumes no falsification, for it goes back to the conditions for the possibility of modern science itself. Ever since Galileo, and metaphysically with Descartes, the human mind postulates that "when we consider things in the order that corresponds to our knowledge of them, our view of them must be different from what it would be if we were speaking of them in accordance with how they exist in reality."[4] The conditions for certain and evident knowledge

---

[4] René Descartes, *Regulae ad directionem ingenii*, in *The Philosophical Writings of Descartes*, vol. 1, tr. John Cottingham, Robert Stoothoff, and Dugald Murdoch (Cambridge: Cambridge University Press, 1985), p. 44.

refer things to the *mens humana*, to the point of distinguishing them from the essence, as it were, that constitutes them in themselves. The *object* takes the place of the *essentiae solitariae*, whose solitude still echoes, from afar, the οὐσία χωριστὴ of Aristotle,[5] for whom the thing defined itself by the uncertain play of the intelligible εἶδος and the material idiocracy: the pure intersection of epistemological parameters that are perfectly intelligible, because totally abstracted from all that does not satisfy, precisely, the conditions of intelligibility itself. The object is not merely defined by relation to the *mens* (*res sibi objecta,* Descartes says);[6] it reflects the *mens* and essentially prolongs it, as its first product. It is because it reproduces the *mens* that the object is its product. "Reification of a theorem": this apt expression should not be limited to scientific experiment, but should be extended to the theoretical object of modern science. Henceforward, the essence of technology appears to precede the empirical practice of the technologies. In other words, the various technologies would not produce any (technological) object if, first of all, the essence of technology—science as method, and not as contemplation of *ousia*—did not constitute the parameters of clear and distinct knowledge as sole reality. In short, technology, considered in its essence, deploys a rationality that depends entirely on the *ego cogitans*. When related to the inversion of the ethical *du sollst!* in totalitarianism, this conclusion strengthens and completes the picture ideology allowed us to glimpse. If ideology does not collapse like a dream awakened, this is not only because constraint, which it justifies theoretically, helps out by backing it up with force. It is above all because the totalitarian model can arise technologically: the development of capacities for economic production through technological progress accordingly enlarges the latitude of state planning; and "planification" (precisely: the ideology of the Plan) is then all the better able to receive what totalitarianism intends. Which implies, inversely, that

---

[5] Descartes, *Regulae,* p. 21.
[6] Descartes, *Regulae,* p. 47.

the choice in favor of an economic and technological development that is as rapid and urgent as possible, even if it originally appears untouched by any ideological implication, can require an ideology to come along and justify its violence: production in effect supposes the substitution of one universe (planned, calculated, and in principle radically intelligible) for another—the world, precisely; technological and economic development can be deployed only when justified in their very violence; and this multiform ideology exists often.

Technical and ideological, morality changes from universal to particular, from formal to concrete, from categorical to hypothetical. Henceforth, how can it impose itself on the moral consciousness? It cannot, and for that matter, does not want to. It is enough if it imposes itself on consciousness (even nonmoral) by the violent and/or rational constraints of ideology and technology. The amoral morality of ideology imposes itself on subjects and is justified in its own eyes (if not in theirs) as precisely what it is—the potency of a power. Power here assumes the collective interplay of technology, ideology, and sometimes (often?) violence. But this very establishment ruins ethics: if the injunction is justified only as a power, power is enough for an utterance to become normative; in short, any utterance whatsoever can become normative so long as a power guarantees it and in light of the fact that no utterance can, on its own, lay claim to being imperative. Ethics goes down in the equivalence of utterances, where power does not challenge it so much as *annul* it.

HATRED AND DISRESPECT

But the transgression of transgression goes even further. Or rather, the equality of utterances already presupposes that the imperative no longer exerts itself over the, from this moment, moral consciousness as an irreducibly exterior authority. Morality becomes hypothetical—and thus particular, multiple and equivalent—only insofar as it first ceases to exert an imperative; it submits to the external condition of a power only insofar as it loses its autonomous *imperium*. How does it lose it, and for that matter, what exactly does it lose in this way? In Kantian terms, the moral law imposes itself imperatively by a twofold authority. Fundamentally, morality imposes itself on reason as such; in its pure formality, the principle "Act in such a manner that the maxim of your will can always be at the same time the principle of a universal act of legislation" states reason as abstract and universal. In hearing it state itself in this manner, man recognizes reason and can thus acknowledge the reasonableness of the reason within him. The requirements set forth by the critique of pure reason had limited the ambitiousness of what reason could lay claim to by restricting reason to the understanding, which, in order to know objectively, must submit to the limits of sensibility. In the ethical imperative, on the contrary, reason can finally achieve the full range of its capacity to be exercised in the unconditional of the purely noumenal. The moral imperative therefore does not exert any constraint, but prompts a recognition of reason. From the simply rational point of view, our age can no longer admit such a recognition, for a reason treated earlier: whereas for Kant reason is equal to universality (and rational morality draws its supreme dignity from it), the reason outfitted by technology and ideology is today no longer practiced except as particular, or broken up into determinate and rival contents. Reason no longer has any other power besides its always partial domination—effective because partial. For us, whether it concerns the work of the concept or, more prosaically, the work of production or of theoretical constraint, reason is put into practice only as nonuniversal, nonformal: all reason is, to us, the reason of something. And if reason imposes nothing, this is because it no longer inspires respect, and our desire is barely even stirred by this fact.

However, from a different, though still Kantian, point of view, a recourse remains. For, concedes Kant, we are not solely made up of reason; constitutively finite minds, we are marked essentially by sensibility, and our will is stirred pathologically. Now, pathologically, the rational imperative can do barely anything, if it can do anything at all. How might it nevertheless impose itself on the pathology of desire? Kant will lay out an analysis that is as powerful as it is paradoxical—that of *respect for the law*.[7] Precisely on account of its being purely rational, the moral imperative humbles the sensibility, whose particularity undergoes the radical critique of the universal: negatively, by the discouragement that it imposes, morality imposes itself on the sensibility; by wounding the sensibility it makes itself felt. The moral law intervenes in person in the sensibility, without, however, making itself sensible. To be sure, in conforming to the desire of my sensibility, I can reject the categorical imperative, but I cannot fail to recognize it, nor can I forget it or slip away from it. That which I refuse, I refuse while recognizing its universality; I can refuse the categorical imperative only by recognizing it, in short by respecting it, and therefore by condemning myself. But we can no longer accept this Kantian response as self-evident. For we no longer have an inevitable respect for the moral injunction. Our desire has in effect learned to distrust reason: it knows that the universal most often hides a determined interest, and that apparently abstract reason aims for a concrete, and therefore self-interested, actuality. In passing to the work of the concept, the appeal loses the abstract transcendence which once inspired respect. Thus, since desire sees itself proposing only a particular maxim, allegedly universal, too, it can oppose to its own particular interest only another particular interest. When choosing between particularities, why not choose the pure subjectivity of individual desire? There is more: the same refusal can come from an opposite motive, for desire can refuse the universal precisely *because* the universal exerts itself as such: why would I respect in someone else the universal reason that

---

[7] Immanuel Kant, *Critique of Practical Reason*, 3d ed., tr. Lewis White Beck (Upper Saddle River, N.J.: Prentice Hall, 1993), pp. 78ff.

makes him Man, when I do not want to recognize myself, an individual ego, in the abstract universal of Man?[8] The universal lacks respect, because I suspect that I am irreducible to the noumenal. Within me, desire wills to be itself, and therefore wills its particularity, and not reason. A maxim stirs me only by remaining particular: I act in a certain way only if the maxim of my action *cannot* become universal law. Desire rejects ethical norms as such because it refuses to let the universal (be it authentic or apparent) judge or limit it; in short, desire does not so much evade the moral norm as *hate* it. If morality deserved the disinterested universality that it lays claim to, if therefore its injunction inspired me with actual respect, wouldn't my freedom require precisely that I hate this universal as such, that, seeing what is best, I have the will *not* to approve it and to turn myself away from it—*meliora video, non probo neque sequor?*

Morality as obedience to a normative injunction would thus become impossible, because its two essential conditions collapse: (1) all norms appear equal and depend, because equally dependent, on the power that gives them strength: thus *indifference* of norms; (2) man does not yield to the norm and obey it, but instead *hates* it, as such.

The Revocation of Ethics

But, it will be objected, is this not an excessively "pessimistic" picture of today's ethical situation? Who has not noticed that many, indeed the majority, still respect a norm and recognize a moral hierarchy of norms? True. But what is the significance of such an observation? It admits at least two interpretations. If morality is, in one way or another, respected, this respect can in no way come from the moral injunction as such, but from constraints imposed by the *power* of the

---

[8] The gap between *me*, as an irreducibly atomic individuality, "idiotic" in the Greek sense, and Man constitutes the essence of Max Stirner's quarrel with B. Bauer and Ludwig Feuerbach; see Stirner, *The Ego and Its Own*, ed. David Leopold (New York: Cambridge University Press, 1995).

norms. The norms of civic morality being infinitely particularized, it falls to political power (whichever it may be) to make them respected. To make the norms respected, to normalize: ideology and technical production speak the same language. To impose concrete norms of morality is, of course, to make a morality respected. But to have to make a morality respected already supposes that the moral injunction as such does not make itself respected, and thus that, though established, it is not worth anything on its own. All morality that must make itself respected by exterior constraints thus admits that it no longer inspires respect by itself—and that it is therefore no longer valid as pure morality. It wills only when imposed by a power that wills it. But one may nonetheless object that, however dominant this situation appears to be (and is), it does not eliminate another authentically moral attitude: namely, that an individual recognize by himself a moral injunction as his absolute norm—in short, that he recognize values. Certainly. But it is precisely the case that, in order to respect these values, one must first of all *will* their respect, and thus must first of all *will* that certain values be ethical norms. The ultimate ground of a theory of (moral) values does not rightly reside in the morality of values, but in the anterior authority which recognizes the values as norms, thus in the will that wills them. That it is a matter here of voluntary servitude changes nothing with regard to the preeminence of the will—it is, precisely, *voluntary* servitude. In this way, the will becomes norm of the norm, just as much in the particular and concrete morality willed by a power (will to *power*) as in the universal and abstract morality willed by a moral conscience (*will* to power). One must therefore conclude that every morality, in its ground, offers one of the possible faces of the will that, by such means, seeks to will itself—the will to power. In the end morality comes down to a will that, in morality, wills only its own enslavement, which wills itself—just like the refusals of morality. This observation reinscribes the bankruptcy of morality in the terminal age of metaphysics, that of nihilism, wherein, according to Nietzsche's thought, the will to power first denies that which is not immediately itself, so as thus to appear as such. Only the will that wills itself remains: the rest, including, above all, morality, affords only the will's symptoms.

Whence this ultimate consequence (though not the last drawn by Nietzsche): if the will to power constitutes every action of man, then indetermination and indifference, which free will suppose, become unthinkable; free will—now a noninnocent illusion—fades before the impeccable conditioning exercised by the will to power. Just as morality resolves itself into an epiphenomenon of the will, freedom of choice gradually resorbs into the necessary and spontaneous affirmation of self by self in which the will to power culminates. Such is the condition that metaphysics grants, at its end, to the ethical impossible.

The metaphysics that has come to its end right before our eyes grants ethics only a single status: revocation. The metaphysical situation does not render the moral act possible: the conditions of its possibility can no longer be thought, because they are contradicted absolutely by power, desire, and the will to power.

The Moral Risk of Not Being Moral

Therefore, we must at least renounce thinking the ethical outside of the practical implementation that an ethical *act* makes of it. Ethics can, perhaps, no longer be thought. But perhaps it does not have to be thought; it has, first, to be actualized; perhaps it is not possible, but at least, as act, it must become actual, with possibility, *indeed even without it.* The act is performed even if thought cannot justify its possibility. Doubtless, one will make objection: certainly, an act can always be accomplished, even if thought does not succeed in thinking its possibility (as in the case of the athlete's extraordinary exploit, the politician's unforeseeable outcome, the gratuitous grace given to the supplicant, and so on); but the properly moral dignity of the act in no way results from such an accomplishment. As an example, take the devotion unto death of a militant for his party, or of a citizen for his country; their resolution can lead them to accomplish the inconceivable; but their devotion unto death, even accomplished, will in no way prove the moral dignity of what they were defending; history has shown frequently that one can die voluntarily for a cause that is partial and biased, arbitrary and imperialistic, perverse and harmful. A cause whose supporters get themselves killed is not sanctified on that account: on the contrary, it condemns itself by their spilled blood. If sacrificing oneself for a cause were enough to sanctify it, history would comprise only good causes, and ethics would be uniformly spread over the face of the earth. This objection hits its mark, but in so doing it shows the path to its own surpassing. If I am confronted with a choice between two attitudes that are equally realizable (or unrealizable, which amounts to the same thing), and I opt for the one that appears to me (in all incertitude, evidently) the least easily reducible to a ruse of desire or a constraint of power, and I accomplish it, can I be sure of a properly ethical action? Evidently not: I know, at a deeper level, that the will to power can—no matter whether it is exerted in my name by another center of will, or in the name of another center through me—determine me without my even being aware. I even know that refusing to affirm oneself immediately as will to power can still depend upon the will to power, which, in its nihilistic form, would rather will nothingness than not will at all. Up until this point, the objection carries. But beyond, it gives way: for what happens if, despite the suspicions consciously borne by my consciousness toward what remains forever unconscious to it, my consciousness persists in deciding to do that which neither desire, nor ability, nor ideology, nor power, nor flesh, nor blood, nor human willing can—directly—decide? The illusion remains, as a risk, but as an accepted risk: the act becomes moral when it assumes the risk of deciding in favor of nonpower through the risk that this nonpower is an illusion. The act becomes moral when it accepts to sacrifice totally its author for, perhaps, the illu-

sion of morality—acting morally is certified when one takes
the risk of losing all for, perhaps, immorality. Moral is the act
that remains so, despite the risk of not being so. Moral is the
act that accepts losing itself in the sole hope, rather than the
assurance, that this loss is moral. The moral act costs so dearly
not on account of the sacrifice but on account of the risk of
sacrificing all for a nonmoral cause. Dying by sacrifice belongs more often to suicide than to devotedness; dying for a
victorious cause, or for whoever loves you, belongs to triumph by proxy more than it does to devotedness; but dying
for a lost cause, and, what is more, for a lost and suspect
cause, belongs either to perversity or to morality. Or to both
at once: when a strictly materialist ideology demands death
for the sake of the party, that is to say demands of a soul that
it give itself freely, it reveals its contradiction, and thus its
perversity; but it also, in spite of itself, allows whoever sacri-
fices himself for this soulless ideology to manifest his soul, for
he proves in dying that he *is* a soul. The martyr does not
prove the morality of the cause; but in dying for a cause that
he accepts as irreducibly doubtful (it is even thus for the
Christian martyr), he proves at the very least his own morality.[9] The party has no soul and kills souls; but in dying for
the party, I prove, against it, indeed against myself, that I am
a soul. Rare are the just (or moral) causes, but numerous the
dead who were worth more than their causes. The dialectic
of mastery and enslavement needs to be written to a second
degree: there, he who accepts the risk of dying in order to
be recognized proves his spirit; here, he who accepts dying
in order to follow the moral injunction, without concealing
from himself the risk of an illusion, proves the morality of
his spirit. In short, the morality of an act derives from the

---

[9] By morality, we understand here not conformity of the act to the
moral requirement (which would oppose morality, in as much as it is
good, to an evil act), but, rather, adherence to the ethical domain as well
as to the domain of freedom (which thus stands in opposition to the totalitarian determination and to *animalitas*). Moral, in this sense, is the act that
enters upon the region in which it becomes possible, beyond power and
ideology, to decide between good and evil.

lucidity of not allowing oneself suspicion as a reason for renouncing morality. Morality involves the increase of lucidity that refuses to make of lucidity itself the criterion of morality.

Moral is the act that chooses to understand itself as moral, at its risk even more than at its peril. Moral is the act that accepts the illusion of being so, and that pays the price, as if there were no illusion involved. Moral is the act that believes in, but does not require the clear vision of, its morality (and therefore exposes itself to a possible immorality).

As If

So where is all of this going? Is this about subjective introspection, which attempts to save moral intention by leaving the field of reason? And to begin with, who would not experience some irritation with the suspect and dangerous imprecision of what we have here been calling "morality"? In fact, we were aiming at a precise result: because the universal domination of the will to power, as absolute reducer of every moral act (by power, ideology, technology, and desire), prohibited access to morality through its theoretical possibility, it was necessary to attempt to win back another concept standing in for morality but transgressing it, through an analysis of the act—even the act whose morality was deeply suspect. It was therefore necessary to mark a gap and to produce a concept. The gap marked was that between what the will to power can reduce and what manifests itself nonetheless: the will to power can reduce all the morality of an act to its own symptoms, but it cannot reduce the assumption of the very risk of this reduction; that is, the will to power can eliminate morality but cannot eliminate one's venture at morality—at self-interpretation as moral rather than as beyond good and evil. The possibility of interpreting the moral act in an extramoral sense designates, rather than disposes of, the counter-possibility of a moral interpretation of this same act. Who will decide the conflict between these two interpretations?

Before any decision, we must first take into account the gap between the two interpretations: even after the reduction exerted by the will to power, I am still free to attempt a moral act, reasonably or not it makes no difference because this freedom de facto belongs to me. In saying this, we have, incidentally, stated the decisive concept substituted for the disqualified concept of morality—*freedom*. In what way am I free? Considered within the network of innumerable hermeneutics and necessities in which power and desire, ideology and technology, planification and production, in short the avatars of the will to power, bind me, I cannot in any way claim myself to be empirically free—free "to do what I will." For precisely, I do not know what I will; indeed, I am infinitely more ill-placed for knowing what I will than are the necessities that master my nonfreedom. But at least I know perfectly well that each act of mine (or even only supposedly mine) will undergo the assault of one reductive hermeneutic or another, which will claim it determined. But here again, I am always still free to oppose a counter-hermeneutic to this reductive hermeneutic: more exactly, I am free to carry on regardless of this first hermeneutic. Let's say that I love a woman, and that I am sure that I love her for herself, and not as part of some fantasy; a thousand interlocutors will reduce what appears to me to be a free and spontaneous impetus to the dissimulated interests of my desire, a function of the relation of force between our respective powers to seduce. Doubtless, I am not free to impugn these reductions, nor even to rid myself *(me défaire)* of their suspicions. But I remain absolutely free to persist in loving this woman. And perhaps in doing so I am abandoning myself to a delirious determinism that ruins me; but might I not also be moving toward happiness? In a sense, the end result does not matter: the only thing that matters here is my freedom to assume the uncertainty. I am free, not because I know the determinations of my choice (Spinoza), nor because I dispense with them absolutely (Kant), but because I can hold them all to be perfectly indifferent. Indifference certainly implies an entitlement to error, but not uniquely (for it may also be the hermeneutic reduction of morality that leads into error). More than an entitlement to error, freedom demands an entitlement to erring. To err—meaning here to advance without markers, rather than to get lost—amounts to freedom, because, in the end, freedom only comes to a decision by itself. If, before the tribunal of ideological and technical power deployed by metaphysical reason, I indisputably lose my freedom along with the morality of my acts, at least there remains to me a freedom to settle myself on living *as if* I were free to make my own decision. Impossible at the first level, freedom remains imprescriptible at the second level: I can decide, against all reason, that in the end it is indeed I who decides for me. *As if* here betrays no lamentable impotence or illusion but instead reveals the distinguished privilege of freedom: without content, it does not admit any prior condition; to act as if I were free signifies that there is never anything lacking for me to act freely—because, precisely, freedom is nothing, it is no being, no cause, no effect, but only what qualifies each comportment with its unreal and absolute modality. If, to act freely, it is enough that I decide to do so—by opposing a counter-hermeneutic to the reduction of a shadowless violence—then I can always render myself free to be free. Nothing is lacking to the *as if*—itself being nothing.

We are thus doubtless taking part in a radical reversal of the relations between freedom and rationality. In metaphysics, rationality determined ethics by stating through concepts its conditions of possibility (or impossibility); in this way, man's freedom was always deduced from theoretical considerations having to do with general being (contingency: Aristotle, Saint Thomas; the absolute: Schelling), with the faculties of the human soul (the will: Descartes; reason: Spinoza, Kant), and its illusions (Nietzsche), with the concept (Hegel), with society, and so forth. In the attempt to separate itself from the will to power, freedom is experienced and won no longer in the wake of rationality but in opposition to it. For if rationality itself today often makes itself totalitarian, it will be quite necessary for freedom to oppose itself to it. From the moment metaphysics no longer assures ethics of its conditions of possibility, it becomes necessary for ethics to ensure for itself its own conditions of possibility. Ethics ensures them only by in turn restoring itself to freedom. In the time of nihilism, ethics coincides with, and in a sense is summed up almost entirely by, freedom. To act morally signifies first of all to prove (oneself) by the decision, lacking any assurance other than an *as if*, that one can act freely. Today we have perhaps no better motive for acting morally than to experiment with freedom, to contradict the totalitarian hermeneutic in all of its transformations.

The Indecision of the Opening

In thus focusing ethics on the experience of freedom, and in particular of a freedom rid of all metaphysical foundation (if by metaphysics one understands the ultimate figure of its destiny: the will to power), do we not run the risk of regressing toward a type of subjective morality? On the contrary. For there is not one experience of freedom, as if man, supposedly known first of all by a nonproblematic definition, subsequently had the experience of freedom as one, among others, of the possible affective states. The inverse is true:

(1) Freedom is not one among many possibilities but, more radically, *the* possible par excellence, in that it opens the very horizon of all that is possible. Freedom renders possible all that is possible as the horizon of all possibilization.[10] Seen in relation to the will to power, which accomplishes itself only by affirming the Eternal Return of the Same, freedom thus becomes its radical denegation: the possibility of what is possible must contradict the return of the Same; it denies the affirmation of the Same because it unceasingly opens the Same to an Other.

(2) Freedom is not counted among man's affective states

---

[10] [Translator's note: *Possibilisation* is a word coined in the French to describe the lifting of something that was impossible to possibility.]

because it no longer depends on a human faculty: the will. The human will deploys itself, in metaphysics, to the point of the will to power, and thereby makes of itself the world; paradoxically, the accomplishment of the will in the will to power removes from man all will, since the will to power itself produces the necessity of the whole. Here, on the contrary, freedom establishes itself beyond every faculty: beyond what reason can admit of or reduce from the will, and eventually beyond the will itself. For freedom does not consist in the use of a faculty—the will—that has been acquired and is available like a tool, but rather in the redoubling, in an unreal manner, of an unreal decision, to the point of opening, according to the *as if*, a pure possibility and no actuality. While the reasoning and reasoned will closes and equips with actuality the horizon of the possible, freedom first frees man from its power, and thus frees the will from power itself; whereas the will to power can only conceal its own rise in power, the decision of the *as if* discloses in the will the possible, which causes it to stand ecstatically outside itself.[11]

(3) Man does not have freedom at his disposal. Rather, freedom exposes man in such a manner that he can never dispense with deciding as if he were acting freely. For such an *as if* does not in any way mark a regression of full freedom, since it defines precisely its unconditional possibility. Freedom institutes man in the absolute unconditionality, which opens all possibility in general, by exposing him to the perfect indigence of the *as if*. Under the desertlike figure of the *as if*, freedom, freed of all presupposition, never fails man; he can always oblige himself to expose himself to the possibility. Every time, and unceasingly, freedom thus precedes my eventual decision to exercise it. Far from his producing it, freedom anticipates man, for it alone opens man to his possibility.

---

[11] Not so much outside the will—which remains the worker, for example, of divinisation—as outside the will conceived as search for the self by itself, will to the *proprium* (Saint Bernard), will to γνώμη (Maximus the Confessor). To think a will that would affirm without affirming itself, that would posit without positing *itself*, that would will without willing *itself* to power, remains a philosophical task as of yet largely unaccomplished.

(4) By these remarks, we arrive at a final paradox. Freedom precedes man, who cannot deduce it from his essence as a property. The *as if* puts into operation this indetermination without any rational or reasonable assurance that I would decide freely. Consequently, freedom does not ground itself in reason *(as if)* because it quite simply does not ground itself, nor does it have need to ground itself. Freedom happens without grounding itself, for if it grounded itself before happening, it would indeed no longer have need to happen, nor could it any longer do so. Therefore freedom eludes all reason. This troubling consequence applies twice. First, to the motive for the decision in the *as if*: because I make my decision without knowing if I am effectively free in this very decision, my decision can produce its motives after the fact just as well as orient itself according to prior reasons; not only do I judge beautiful what I love and because I love it, but my decision modifies decidedly every hermeneutic of my world; the eventual motives thanks to which I may give reason for my use of the *as if* aver themselves to be the shadow projected over the understanding of the decision, itself without reason; I never know what I am doing, nor why I am doing it, during the time in which I do it—if I did know, I would have no need to do it; in this way, freedom always precedes the reasons for being free, since it provokes them. Born of itself, the free decision to act as if I were free appears as the closest and the final undecidable. Within me, freedom, more me than me, anticipates me, decides me within myself as if I were free, and places me before the accomplished deed. I am freedom—because it precedes me. But there is a second corollary to such a lack of reason: because the freedom to be free presupposes no grounding, it cannot seek to resolve what one might like to define as a human essence. The freedom to be free does not belong to the "thinking animal," for neither the λόγος nor the *ratio* nor the *cogitatio* precede it or determine it. Neither does it belong to the will to power, for, in order to will to power, this will (as we have seen) wills power as the auto-foundation that is all the more foundational in that the will identifies itself with this foundation.

Might it belong, then, to the *Dasein* in that, like the *Dasein*, it transcends all thematizable and knowable beings to the point of clearing, by its unconditioned "apertness" *(apérité)*, the opening of Being? In short, does the opening of the decision immediately sketch the opening by the *Dasein* (who thus becomes opening's lieutenant) of beings to Being? Despite the authority of *Sein und Zeit*, it is appropriate to contest the equivalence between these two openings: the freedom to be free, absolutely unconditioned and without any material or ontic determination, offers no indication for identification; neither consciousness nor will to power nor *Dasein* can know it; none of these recognizes itself there at all, for nothing, not even the nothing in which Being announces itself, can pierce through the clearly unmasked *persona* of the *as if*. The freedom to be free redoubles itself without recourse to Being, despite the tale of Being that usage here maintains: free to play itself as free; no obligation, not even that of being, must, in principle, oblige it. Without pursuing here the demonstration of such a freedom without being,[12] let us underscore that the freedom of the *as if* is by right obligatory only according to its own decision, and that, if a name or a place had to secure it a genealogy or a site, this freedom should admit these only as part of its very opening and the requirements of the absolute possibility thus accomplished.

Defined in this way, or rather removed from all definition since it only enters upon its essence by opening itself onto an aseity *(aséité)* without initial or initiating foundation or reason, and not by (de)limiting itself, freedom frees itself not only from ideology, the essence of technology, the will to power, consciousness and even *Dasein*. Beyond these, it accomplishes a reversal without return: the morality induced by the *as if*'s freedom, free of self, rests on no prior theoretical condition, but evades and precedes it. The morality that per-

---

[12] According to the thematic posed by *Dieu sans l'être* (Paris: Presses Universitaires de France, 1991; *God Without Being,* tr. Thomas A. Carlson [Chicago: University of Chicago Press, 1991]), in particular chapter IV.

mits the freedom to be free already establishes by itself an ἦθος, which is deployed without any logical condition. Freedom according to the *as if* does not ripen like the late fruit of a tree rooted metaphysically or phenomenologically; it inaugurates or renders possible possibility itself, slashing with a clean cut the cover veiling the horizon, otherwise open. Thus it finally opens man himself as the unique instance and stake of possibilization in general. Freedom opens the possible to all theory subsequent to and before it. We rediscover, therefore, with the unconditioned freedom of deciding oneself as free, a sort of echo of what Descartes named "a provisional moral code"[13]: before nothing, or even nothingness, comes to guarantee morality or freedom, freedom lays in a supply of its sole *as if*, in order to realize itself, decidedly if not definitively, as pure possibility.

But *who* then can thus discover himself free to decide that he decides freely—for, after this inaugural decision, there is no reason, no foundation, no appeal to illuminate it or lift it to possibility? Of what glory does man, free to be free, bear the anonymous brilliance?

September 1981–August 1986

---

[13] [Translator's note: "une morale par provision," from the *Discourse on Method*, part 3; *The Philosophical Writings of Descartes*, vol. 1, tr. John Cottingham, Robert Stoothoff, and Dugald Murdoch (Cambridge: Cambridge University Press, 1985), p. 122.]

3

Evidence and Bedazzlement

WHEN A SIMPLE-MINDED AND RECURRENT CRITICISM sets itself against the discourse put forth under the name of apologetics, at what does it aim its apparent indictment? Usually, the criticism stigmatizes the claim, supposedly held by the ecclesial intelligentsia, to rigorous proof of the truth of Christianity by means of a compelling conceptual system—an insupportable claim, incidentally, first and above all because it supposes that Christian, and namely Catholic, thought has at its disposal a sufficient conceptual system, thus marking itself with a "triumphalism" worthy of condemnation. The Christian faith would of course have nothing to win by advancing itself with such a train of reasons or arguments, because "poverty" and "self-denial" befit its fundamental humility. Let us put aside the question of whether, historically, the Church might have practiced an apologetics that was triumphal to the point of excess,[1] and whether the humility of charity ne-

---

[1] For the most part, it is legitimate to doubt this. Indeed, in the most significant case, Roman authority spoke plainly: G. Hermes (1775–1831) held (among others, in *Einleitung in die christkatholische Theologie,* Münster 1819) that each point of revelation could and should be the object of a rational demonstration, and that, while awaiting such demonstration, the employment of a positive doubt was legitimate. This position, tending to collapse the "content" of faith into the "means" of believing, was expressly condemned by Gregory XVI (*Dum acerbissimas,* 1835; Denzinger, *Enchiridion Symbolorum,* n. 1619; etc.). This condemnation obviously does not contradict in any way the affirmation of Vatican I that God *certo cognosci posse* (Denziger 1785, 1806), inasmuch as this certainty concerns God as *rerum omnium principium et finem,* as *creatorem et Dominum nostrum,* that is to say, God as manifested by the *visibilia,* and not in the definitive figure of Christ. The argumentation remains strictly rational, because the revelation of God as Love has not yet entered in. But a finally Christic apologetics must go all the way to this last point.

cessitates the cultivation of intellectual wretchedness; let us instead ask if such an attitude does not lead, with regard to apologetics, to a surreptitious recuperation, and also to a theological misunderstanding.

NONAPOLOGETICS

A recuperation: ostensibly renounce all preparation or rational confirmation of faith, and thus assure the non-Christian or "atheistic" (as we think we can say) interlocutor that we will not deploy against him any argumentative machine (because we lack one), and that his identity will thereby be perfectly respected (even if the obliging Christian risks losing his own)—such an approach has at least one consequence. The Christian, clearly having withdrawn from all intellectual imperialism, no longer disturbs the "conflict of ideas" (even if, in another sense, he can become bothersome by dint of his smiling pusillanimity); he stands there in his place, and nowhere but his place. The renunciation of all apologetics *can* also facilitate the Christian's warm welcome into his cultural surroundings and permit him to be accepted. But how then does nonapologetics differ, as to its result, from apologetics? Certainly, such good will must come at the price of a certain weakness: it is an already almost anonymous Christian, because without theology, if not without Church, that those who tolerate being called "anonymous Christians" will admit into their circle, because their benevolent commiseration knows perfectly his inoffensive and childish impoliteness. Nevertheless, a difference remains: apologetics, with its reasons, attempts to gain Christ's admittance (at the risk of the Christian's being poorly received), while nonapologetics, free of reasons, tries to gain the "Christian's" reception (at the price, sometimes, of Christ's not being admitted). The aim of convincing, or at least of trying to please, is the same for both; the point of application has simply been displaced. One might surmise, then, that the change in attitude toward apologetics reflects a conceptual displacement in dogmatics, and that the renunciation of constructed apologetic discourse should be recognized according to decidedly conceptual themes: to a dogmatics that is suffering from mounting difficulties (at least in France) in defining both its epistemological status and, above all, the irreducible and specific primacy of the "Christianity" of the Christic fact, there can obviously correspond only a nonapologetics, which perhaps no longer has at its disposal even the means to sustain a dialogue with anyone at all. Such continuity between dogmatics and apologetics stands out, then, all the better because the same negative index, at times, seems to affect them; in what we are considering here, this point says much, for it signals a new status for apologetics. The aim would no longer be (but has this ever been the goal?) to develop an argumentative machine, which would claim, like well-executed propaganda, to force an intimate conviction by force of reasons, or rather of popular slogans, an approach that testifies more to a will to dominate and strengthen an apparatus, than to a gesture of love revealing Love. Rather, the aim would be the external expansion of what shapes, lifts, and incites dogmatics from the depths of itself, or rather from the depths of what convokes and institutes it: the tremendous and incompressible δύναμις τοῦ θεοῦ that exposes its explosion in liturgy, contemplation, and dogmatic theology, in order to be carried on naturally in apologetics, supposing of course that a perfect, humble, and poor availability toward the Spirit of God poured out in our hearts is natural. Apologetics does not so much constitute a discipline other than dogmatics, nor even its prolongation or its pastoral transcription, as it offers the index of the impregnation by the power of God of theological meditation as a whole. For a thought's power of conviction rests not so much in the energy of the zealot (the militant compensates for the inanity of the slogan with his indiscrete zeal, just as the ad-man supports the uselessness of his product with his "marketing strategy"), as it does in the power of the thought. How much more so if this thought comes to us from He who "sustains all things by the power of his word" (Hebrews 1:3).

Necessary Failure

We have risked a theological misunderstanding, and for a reason. The spiritual relation of expansion between dogmatics and apologetics becomes unrecognizable as soon as one believes that one can fix as the goal of apologetics to convince, necessarily and by reasons. From this first hypothesis, two choices appear. Either (and this is at present the most widespread case) apologetics appears useless, because its goal—to convince, or at least to "open a dialogue"—can be reached by other means than reasons; the confiding exchange of opinions, the silent community of experiences, the sharing of hopes and struggles, in a word the irrational of "lived experience," would allow much more efficiently for the convincing of those who are not Christian of the truth of the God who is revealed in Jesus Christ, or at least for the admittance of oneself as a Christian among them. But such silence, in its refusal to speak, already says too much: it implies that faith, in order to transmit itself, requires neither speech nor listening (in opposition to Romans 10:14–18), and thus that, finally and quite logically, faith does not transmit itself at all. With this assertion, an "invention of faith" must be supposed, the speaking of which does not happen without an uproar, and implies once again one or several discourses in dogmatic theology. Dogmatic theology will have to justify the apologetic silence, whose taciturnity will often appear gregarious, by dint of explanations. Thus we find ourselves brought to the other possibility: apologetics can hold the sense of being able to convince necessarily through demonstrations; this temptation certainly does not have priority among the threats menacing us at this time, but its current disappearance perhaps reflects our situation all the better, because such was for a long time its aim, and this aim no doubt remains operative in the sharpest current criticisms of apologetics. Let us suppose—in what is an extreme and unthinkable case—that an apologetic discourse were to attain such a degree of rigor that it could claim to convince necessarily a normally rational mind. What result would in fact have been gained? The voluntary moment of adherence would come up only as a simple consequence of the evidence, by a sort of moral necessity, following the principle that from a great light in the understanding there follows a great inclination in the will. What is called "conversion" is played out precisely in this consequence, which ought to be self-evident, and which, most of the time, seems all the less self-evident, exactly because the proofs claim to have established their result. Who has not come across these minds who, fine connoisseurs of dogmatics and Christian spirituality, intellectually disposed to expound them and justify them, never cease their whole life long to avoid the consequences and to dodge, by the inky cloud of a limitless sympathy, the adversity of a faith decision? So long as the will does not freely will to love, apologetics has gained nothing. Consequently, in not recognizing the most decisive factor, an apologetics that means to be absolutely demonstrative would, by its very success, be condemned to the most patent failure. What can be demonstrated has no value, Nietzsche claimed; for in saying it all and even too much, we say infinitely too little. Renouncing apologetics, like succeeding in it, leads to failure. Why?

Because apologetics does not correctly understand its office insofar as it claims *to convince* necessarily and through reasons, where it should claim only *to constrain* (unless it aims to constrain where it should instead hope to convince). Let us be more precise: a constraint is legitimately tolerable only where its exercise does not introduce any heteronomy. In such a case, the reasons that an argument assembles can constrain reason because reason in such a case still follows only its own necessity. If, then, apologetics laid claim only to rational evidence, it could, supposing it had the means, be content with constraint, that is to say, with leading a mind, necessarily, to the end of a demonstration. But apologetics is concerned with something wholly other: to convince. To convince supposes a new factor, the will (or whatever one wants to call the ultimate compelling cause of existential decision), which decides—that is to say, decides for itself on the

basis of itself alone, such that all other causal authority appears exterior and therefore ineffectual, whether it claims to
be threatening or helpful. Only the will can allow itself to be
convinced, and all constraint of reason by reasons remains
totally heterogeneous to it, remains on the threshold and decides nothing. Apologetics, in using reasons alone, can, in
the best of cases, constrain reason; but even in this event, it
will not for all that convince the will, and will fail in its duty
at the precise moment when it believes it is fulfilling it. As
for confusing everything, and hoping to constrain the will,
because reasons cannot do it, one can aspire to do so only by
having recourse to force; but force, no matter how subtle it
might be, emphasizes and confirms all the more the exteriority of its violence, which it never stops extending. If it wants
to leave nothing outside rational constraint, apologetics loses
any adherence of the will, which alone can allow itself to be
convinced. In short, it is only by admitting the irreducible
gap between constraint (of reason by reasons) and conviction
(of the will by itself) that apologetics recognizes its proper
task, which begins beyond any demonstration. Not only
when demonstration reveals itself to be impossible, but also
when it seems fully established. For it is then up to the will
to let itself be convinced, in its heart of hearts. Thus, because
it accedes to its proper task, apologetics finds itself destitute:
without reasons, for by right all the sufficient reasons in the
world do not suffice to convince a will. In clearly distinguishing constraint from conviction, apologetics runs up
against its originality and its destitution: it becomes possible
as such only in admitting the impossibility of a necessary success. Its identity coincides with its failure.

REASON AND WILL

But what does it mean here to fail? This term makes sense
only so long as we think of apologetics in terms of a model
that has become null and void—the rational method for
constraining the will by reasons. Once this paradigm has

been contested, the same impossibility could, from another
point of view, be interpreted wholly otherwise, no longer as
a deficiency, but as a superabundance. How? If the conviction of the will by itself passes decidedly beyond the constraint of reason by reasons, this is above all because the will
(or whatever one wants to call the compelling cause of the
ultimate decision) surpasses the play of reasons. The fact that
reasons cannot constrain the will reveals its superabundance,
its *exsuperentia*. To speak here of any sort of irrationalism
would still suppose that reason holds a normative value. And
to conceive of the excess of the will as the importation of
the metaphysical concept of will (will to power for example)
would perhaps only increase the confusion, since the will to
power constitutes, for Nietzsche and the metaphysics completed in him, the truth of reason itself; thus the will annuls
as well as completes itself, as it were in its essence, in the will
to power.[2] Will here indicates less a faculty, an attribute, or a
power for existential decision making than the compelling
cause about which Pascal says that "the will naturally loves,"
while the mind "*naturally believes*," that is to say emits and
admits opinions or truths (*Pensées* Br. §81/L. 661).[3] The irreducible irruption of the will marks the inconceivable and
discontinuous passage from evidence to love. Between the
evidence of reasons and the will of faith, the passage leads
from one order to another. If then we know the truth not
only by reason but also by the heart (*Pensées*, Br. §82/L. 44),
it is because only the heart can reach the ultimate truth, that
alone which is not a figure of something else, that alone
which symbolizes itself: charity. Reasons, as constraining and
rigorous as they might be, are capable of nothing when it is

---

[2] See, for example, *Thus Spoke Zarathustra*, II: "On the Famous Wise
Men," in *The Will to Power*, tr. Walter Kaufmann (New York: Viking
Press, 1962), p. 298; Fragment 9 [91] in Nietzsche, *Werke*, ed. Colli and
Montinari (Berlin: Walter de Gruyter, 1970), vol. VIII/2, p. 48. The will
to power does not annul rationality but, by understanding it in its essence
as will to truth, it carries it to completion under the nihilistic figure of the
essence of technology.

[3] [Translator's note: English renditions of Pascal come from Blaise Pascal, *Pensées*, tr. A. J. Krailsheimer (Harmondsworth: Penguin, 1966).]

a question of reaching as a fact of truth that which has the name charity, for "All bodies together and all minds together and all their products are not worth the least impulse of charity. This is of an infinitely superior order. . . . Out of all bodies together we could not extract one impulse of true charity. It is impossible and of a different, supernatural order" (*Pensées*, Br. §793/L. 308). The will passes beyond reason constrained by reasons only insofar as the order of charity infinitely, supernaturally transcends the order of minds. Must it be repeated that the so-called argument of the wager is entirely organized around emphasizing this imbalance? Its difficulty does not in the least stem from the rigor of the reasoning, which constrains conceptually—"This is conclusive and if men are capable of any truth this is it" (*Pensées*, §233/418); rather, it comes from the gap that Pascal himself emphasizes with insistence: if the libertine retracts, it is not because the argument can constrain him, but to the contrary precisely because, constraining the reason in him, the argument drives him to the brink of considering a decision of the will: "I am being forced to wager and I am not free; I am being held fast and I am so made that I cannot believe" (*Pensées*, §233/418). The libertine cannot debate the argumentation. It is thus necessary that he carry the debate to its real place—a debate about the will, which must love. To make God known to reason, if the will does not want to acknowledge him, serves no purpose, except to confuse the will's ill will (in the strict sense). Apologetics aims only to lead man to this precise point and this unavoidable debate: to leave the will sufficiently free of itself (and without a loophole in the rational discussion) to admit that the love of God, God as love, is to be loved voluntarily or refused. When for each response the libertine hears himself say: "Concentrate then not on convincing yourself by multiplying proofs of God's existence but by diminishing your passions" (*Pensées*, §233/418), it is not a matter of regressing back from reason, but rather of rendering the will able to want love. *"S'abêtir,"* to make oneself dumb: this advice counsels neither stupidity (Victor Cousin), nor the least bit of skepticism (Léon Brunschvicq); it does not urge taking refuge, nor hiding, in reason, where the will is only playing with itself. The will alone can love, and reasons cannot in any way, by their superabundant constraint, exempt the will from deciding. In short, because "there is a great distance between the knowledge of God and loving him" (*Pensées*, Br. §280/L.377), only the will can love that which reason knows, without, by definition, being able to do better than knowing. Rigorously, if "God is love" (John 3:8), then love alone—and thus the will—will be able to reach him.

No doubt there are gods that love does not essentially characterize, and of which it is only a matter of knowing. Such gnosis perhaps suits the "God of the philosophers and learned men," but in matters concerning the "God of Abraham, Isaac, and Jacob," who reveals himself in Jesus Christ as love, love alone is suitable for reaching him. Perhaps this is so because like knows like, but above all it is true because "the love of God has been poured into our hearts by the Holy Spirit which is given to us" (Romans 5:5): in knowing God by the loving act of the will, man imitates God in his highest name (Dionysius, *Divine Names* XIII, 3; *Patrologia Graeca,* J.-P. Migne, ed., 3, 981a), and becomes, by the grace of love, himself God. God is approached only by he who jettisons all that does not befit love; God, who gives himself as Love only through love, can be reached only so long as one receives him by love, and to receive him by love becomes possible only for he who gives himself to him. Surrendering oneself to love, not surrendering oneself to evidence. Thus, apologetics in no way has as its function the filling of the abyss of the voluntary decision for or against Love, by some conceited expansion of arguments; such a function would be meaningless and contradictory. On the contrary, in settling as quickly and as well as possible the theoretical debate, apologetics plays the role of clearly indicating the place where the decision of the will must intervene, so that the will might know what it must, without avoidance, accept or refuse, and above all that the will might know the One whom it must repudiate or confess. Paradoxically, apologetics should aim only *to reinforce* the difficulty, by situating it at its real and genuine dignity: faith neither compensates for the lack of evidence nor resolves itself in arguments, but decides by the will for or against the love of Love. The point of apologetics is thus to lead, by the constraint of reasons, to this place where, finally, the "heart," faced with the eventual evidence of truths, passes across evidence to Love. For each of us believes alone (that is, in the eyes of the world—in fact, each of us believes only from within the bosom and by virtue of the Church), just as each of us dies alone (again, according to the world's view—for, in fact, each of us dies in the company of the singular and eternal sufferer of Gethsemane); to accomplish the ultimate transition, or to declare oneself either proudly incapable of, or miserably exempted from, undertaking it, each of us finds himself radically solitary, abandoned in a sense by God himself. Thus it is that Good Friday remains the paradigm of all conversion, death to self, filial resurrection in the Father. Apologetics culminates at the threshold of Love, which only love can cross with an unbalanced step that singularly starts us off, and which is often experienced as a fall. Apologetics aims to let the uneasy believer alone, faced with his fear, his love, and the will that oscillates between the two. The failing of apologetics completes itself in the failing through which it abandons love (or refusal) to Love. Nonetheless, apologetics authenticates itself as Christian in these fraternal failures.

The Smallest of Abysses

But an objection immediately arises. In thus delimiting its field and its scope, our analysis indeed gives to apologetics a theological rigor more worthy of the Love in which God gives himself; but such an acquisition comes at a high price: the unsettled believer finds himself abandoned to a power of greater seriousness, now that he recognizes it often and understands it to be necessary. What does it matter that deficiency theologically authenticates apologetics, if this authenticity comes at the cost of a failure that cannot be overcome! What answer do we give to he who objects (and we have all said or heard this admission): "I don't have the faith that I wish I had; or, I have the unbelief that I wish I didn't have"? Nothing—there is no answer to give, and for several reasons. First, such a formulation is given as an objection, therefore as an argument, and attempts, be it only unconsciously, to make the stake of the will once again into a discussion of reasons, thereby risking the concealment of the infinite distance between the orders. Second, even if this is not a denial in the form of an argument, it can only be an observation—perfectly accurate, though sorrowful—of the fact that, as we are used to saying, faith is a grace. But this too must be understood correctly. What does it mean not to have enough faith? At the very least, that the will does not have the strength to will and that it cannot will, even though it seems to want to. The will hopes to surmount this lack of will, unless it is resigned to it as an excellent pretext for justifying its denial, by some sort of exterior addition of a supplement of will. When Senancour objects to Pascal by asking, "Has believing ever depended on the will?"[4] he merely and indirectly suggests that the fact of believing depends on the will, albeit in its perfect fulfillment, in contrast to its common manifestation. Now, such supplemental assistance inevitably introduces a heteronomy, which, in filling the demand, would radically disqualify the deficient will at the very moment of helping it; external help would in effect forbid the will from accomplishing the very thing that is asked of it—to love Love—by removing its responsibility in the very fact of furnishing it with means foreign to it. Nothing can be substituted, even partially, for the will in its dispute with Love, for nothing constitutes man more essentially than

---

[4] "The great Pascal said something puerile when he said, 'Believe because you risk nothing in believing, and because you risk a great deal in not believing.' This reasoning is decisive, if it is a question of conduct; it is absurd when it is faith one is speaking about. Has believing ever depended on the will?" Etienne Pivert de Senancour, *Oberman*, "Lettre XLIV" (Paris: Hachette, 1965), p. 197.

the "heart." To modify a will, even with the goal of increasing it, and even if it is deficient, would amount to alienating it, and thus also to annulling the theological standing of its willing. The will must therefore grow with its little bit of faith, and with it alone, for this little bit of faith alone constitutes it as unique and irreducible.

Alone with itself, the will must will to believe, even when it lacks the means for believing, or rather, when it does not believe the means are available to it. For what holds the will back from believing is believing that it cannot believe, or, in a word, believing that it does not believe. Nothing separates, perhaps, he who believes from he who does not believe, except this: not reasons, of course, not some certainty (as if it were a matter of some sort of nervous or magical influx, near to fanaticism or unconscious stupidity), but merely believing despite the belief that one does not believe. To believe in Love, and that Love loves me in spite of my belief that "I don't have faith"; in other words, to put more confidence in the Love that is given than in our deficient will; to compensate the distrust in oneself with trust in God; to prefer the immensity of the gift proposed (at the risk of failure to receive it through lack of *capacitas*) to the certainty of assumed impotence (at the price of suicide by a self-satisfaction resigned to nothingness); to make up one's mind in favor of the infinite that one cannot master or possess rather than the dandy's impotence; to risk abandon to the overabundance of a gift, instead of immobilizing oneself in the idiocracy of scarcity. Nothing separates the believer from the unbeliever, except faith, which plays out over nothing: *nothing*, which is here a way to say the oscillation of the will in front of Love. The badly believing or unbelieving will lacks not the exterior contribution of some alienating will, but its own transvaluation in love: no longer to will (in order) to affirm itself and thus to master a possession, which would be empty if assured, but to will (in order) to abandon itself to distance, traveled over, received, and unsurpassable. To believe, the will needs only *to will otherwise*: to abandon itself to the gift, instead of assuring itself of a possession. To believe, the will needs only to convert. Nothing separates it from faith but love. Before this smallest of abysses, not only does the will remain alone, but it must renounce its solitude, undo itself from its idiotic solitude, strictly, in order to lose itself in the alterity where, with the other who is found always already there, one enters into distance. Grace, in this play, does not intervene as a surplus, illegitimate and incomprehensible, but as a new modality (*tropos,* says Maximus Confessor)[5] of this same will. Thus grace constitutes the most proper depth of the will—*interior intimo meo*—as well as its most intimate stranger.[6]

BEDAZZLEMENT

Still, when defined thus, apologetics would appear to lead from evidence to obscurity, and to rely on the irrational. But apart from the fact that the domain of the will, being here radically foreign to the order of reasons, remains thus also unharmed by any irrationality, the nature of the obscurity at issue here still must be correctly understood. On this condition alone, this obscurity will be able to enter upon another clarity. If "God does not manifest himself to men as obviously as he might" (*Pensées,* §556/449), no doubt this is in order to indicate to the will its particular and fitting task, but especially it is because, just as "first principles have much too

---

[5] On this precise point, see among others Juan Miguel Garrigues, *Maxime le Confesseur: la charité, avenir divin de l'homme* (Paris: Beauchesne, 1976), and Jean-Luc Marion, "Les deux volontés du Christ selon saint Maxime le Confesseur," *Résurrection* 41 (1972).

[6] The analysis of the deficiency of the will, and then of its conversion, would have to be set forth in terms of Augustine, *Confessions* VIII, particularly 19–30. The *lux securitatis* floods the heart that doubts only after it has accepted to come (*surrexi, redii*) and read the words of Saint Paul. This is why the quarrel over the historical character of the story is not, from the theological point of view, decisive: what counts is less the origin of the themes and more their use and their classification for signifying the deficient will. In another style, one could evoke Blondel; see Marion, "La conversion de la volonté selon *L'Action,*" *Revue Philosophique* 177 (1987): 33–46.

much evidence for us" (*Pensées*, §72/199), so too what Jesus Christ reveals of God shows much too much evidence for our gaze. For if God opts for "the presence of a hidden God" (*Pensées*, §449/156), this is because no other presence would remain bearable: no mortal can see him without dying, no eye can fix on his shining forth without blinding itself in such a bedazzling sight. What blindness interprets as a simple obscurity must be understood at base as a bedazzlement, in which, in the revelatory figure of Jesus Christ, the Father enters into an absolute epiphany, though filtered through finitude. If blindness sees nothing there and does not even suspect bedazzlement, the fault lies not with revelation, but with the gaze that cannot bear the evidence. In effect, if what reveals itself is always summed up in Love, then only the gaze that believes, and thus only the will that loves, can welcome it.[7] Thus only the conversion of the gaze can render the eye apt to recognize the blinding evidence of love in what bedazzles it. Standing before Christ on the Cross, who contains in Himself all the prophecies, and who a placard identifies—in three languages!—as the King of the Jews, those who do not accept to love him see nothing, except the confirmation of their denial; those who do love him (the "good thief," Mary, John, the soldier of Mark 15:34) see, with a clarity that is variable to be sure but always indisputable, the highest figure of God, royal in his *kenosis*. The same single figure thus provokes this ambivalence, not because it is itself weighted with the least ambiguity, but because each mind uses its own measure to interpret it. This measure is

---

[7] See *Pensées*, §564/835: "There is enough evidence to condemn and not enough to convince, so that it should be apparent that those who follow it are prompted to do so by grace and not by reason, and those who evade it are prompted by concupiscence and not by reason"; see also *Lettre IV aux Rouannez*: "If God revealed Himself continually to men, there would be no merit at all in believing in Him; if He never revealed Himself, there would be no faith. But ordinarily He conceals Himself, and He reveals Himself but rarely to those whom He wishes to engage in His service" (*Oeuvres Complètes*, ed. L. Lafuma [Paris: Editions du Seuil, 1963], p. 267; Emile Caillet and John C. Blankenagel, tr., *Great Shorter Works of Pascal* [Philadelphia: Westminster Press, 1948], p. 146).

defined by what the gaze can bear; for simply in order to see a figure (that is, to let a figure constitute itself in the realm of the visible), it behooves us first to bear its brilliance, to support the sight of it. As when confronted with the obscene (the menacing as well as the forbidden), the divine, and above all the *kenosis of the Son*, our gaze cannot remain fixed; it blinks and closes. It finds too much to see there, too much to envisage and look at squarely, and, thus, too much to interpret and to allow to interpret us, and so it flees; our furtive gaze turns away from and deserts the visible whose effrontery threatens us. In short, our gaze deserts, and closes. Only love, "which bears all" (1 Corinthians 13:7), can bear with its gaze Love's excess. In proportion to our love, our gaze can open, be it only by blinking, to the evidence of Love. In this proportion also, bedazzlements can become evidence, by the simple fact that we can envisage upholding them. But once again, only love can bear certain sights without flinching: the suffering of a mind that is in bodily agony, the nakedness of a body rendered spiritual by its fullness of pleasure, God's abandon in the manifested form of a humanity.

This indeed is why one always begins in apologetics with the weakest evidence possible, which requires a small investment of love to be seen and thus interpreted; one begins, at the threshold, with arguments based on fact (Jesus historically lived; he claimed divinity, and was put to death for it; a community believed in his resurrection to the point of likewise risking its life; for twenty centuries, his disciples have remained)—the weakest possible evidence precisely because it "calls upon" each and every one without demanding a choice or an answer. Then apologetics proposes other arguments that, in demanding a growing degree of interpretation, enjoin a greater effort from the gaze (for instance, the completion of the prophecies, the meaningful succession of historical events, and so on), until, at its limit, it culminates in the ultimate bedazzlement, before which any human gaze, as loving as it may be, will never stop blinking until the Holy Spirit qualifies it absolutely and permits it to receive bedazzlement as an unsurpassable evidence, that is, as a proof (in the English sense of the word): the Resurrection, absolute theophany. In this sense only, then, does faith have proofs at its disposal, yet these are proofs upon which faith does not rest, for only faith can see them; a fact by which these proofs escape radically from any suspicion of "subjectivism."

One thus comes to understand that the fundamental arguments escape the domain of current apologetics: not because current apologetics lacks them, but because interlocutors who would not give way before them are lacking. The failure of apologetics is therefore justified in a second sense by the failure of the human gaze, frenetically resigned to its limits, stuck to death on its blissful impotence, proudly fixed in its own lack of ambition—in front of the fullness of the visible. There are things that M. Homais[8] will, perhaps, never see, in the sense that, in front of a Mont Sainte-Victoire from the later Cézanne, many an inattentive visitor, as it is said, *"n'y voit que du feu"* (can make neither heads nor tails of it, that is to say, does not even see the fire that Cézanne, who stopped working the theme in the middle of the day, tried to remove from it).[9] In thus giving way, apologetics again confirms that love alone accedes to Love, because

---

[8] [Translator's note: the type personified by the scientistic bourgeois pharmacist Homais in Gustave Flaubert's *Madame Bovary*.]

[9] It is here no doubt that it becomes possible to indicate the epistemological status (if one dares speak thus) of apologetic arguments: *fitness*. Fitness does not indicate a regression from the demand for rigor, but a mode of rigor adapted to that with which it is concerned: the organization of facts according to a scheme more and more saturated with meaning as the arguments touch more on the human (and the divine). The more the superabundance of meaning increases, the more the logic used must be resorbed into what is fitting. Fitness culminates in the interpretation of the Paschal *triduum*, when Christ interpreting himself (*diermeneusen*, Luke 24:27) shows that it was "necessary [*edei, oportuit*] that the Christ suffer these things and enter into his glory" (Luke 24:26). But it is precisely the superiority of fitness that he who does not love and whose "eyes are kept from recognizing him" (Luke 24:26) cannot follow. Fitness becomes clarifying only if the "foolish men, slow of heart to believe" (Luke 24:25) let "their eyes open" (Luke 24:30) before the sign of charity. This is why, once their eyes are open, Christ can disappear bodily: a greater evidence fills the gaze.

only the gaze that bears the visible can abandon itself to the infinite depths of the Christ, Paschal icon of the Father. Grasped as the instance which, propadeutically, helps to see, apologetics indeed appears as a machine, not, of course, for making gods (Bergson), but for making, along with blindness, evidence, provided at least—and this is not its job—that love opens the eyes. Opens the eyes: not in the way violence opens the eyes of the disabused, but as a child opens his eyes to the world, or a sleeper opens his eyes to the morning.

Confirmed by its twofold failure, apologetics can recover a theological legitimacy, as a style of phenomenology (but strictly foreign to philosophy) of the mind laboring at conversion. It therefore progresses toward its goal—to reach Love by love—only by becoming useless (as regards arguments) little by little, for finally love alone, and not discourse, can go to the place where apologetics claims to lead. Its voluntary and progressive disappearance implies less its renunciation and more its slow transformation in the confession of faith: the catechumen will one day say the *Credo* and take part in the Eucharist, that is to say, will profess He whom he will have received. From preparatory apologetics, he will pass to the believer's apology of faith, the form of witnessing which, in the first centuries, was called apology: "Make a defense [apology] before the people" (Acts 19:33). This suggests less a demonstration than an acknowledgement of the Resurrected, of "him with whom we have to do" (Hebrews 4:13), by pleading on behalf of the well-foundedness and rightfulness of his Gospel. Nothing will ever exempt the Church from apologetics thus understood, except risking apostasy. For in apologetics, it is less an issue of our access to God, than of his coming to us: "Being able to demonstrate God is not sufficient for reaching him, for God exceeds his own 'demonstrability.' One can execute the proof of God to the point of absurdity; it will never come to an end. Its terminal point is a leap, a burst of the love of God toward his creature, which makes the under-

standing burst forth for the sake of facing up to faith in love"
(Adrienne von Speyr).[10] But the passage from one sense of
apologetics to the other constitutes in the end its meaning
and its significance.

May 1978

[10] Adrienne von Speyr in the anthology presented by Hans Urs von Balthasar, *Adrienne von Speyr et sa mission théologique* (Paris: Éditions de la Mais-
nie, 1976), text 23 (drawn from the commentary on John 3:16), p. 116.
In other words, it is a question of "understanding all proofs as [an] initia-
tion into incomprehensibility," as Karl Rahner puts it in *Foundations of
Christian Faith: an Introduction to the Idea of Christianity*, tr. William V. Dych
(New York: Seabury Press, 1978), p. 125 (translation modified).

4

The Intentionality of Love

In homage to Emmanuel Lévinas

WE LIVE with love as if we knew what it was about. But as soon as we try to define it, or at least approach it with concepts, it draws away from us. We conclude from this that love ought not and cannot be conceived accurately, that it withdraws from all intelligibility, and that every effort to thematize it belongs to sophistry or an unseemly abstraction. The inevitable consequence of this attitude is self-evident: we can give love only an interpretation, or rather a noninterpretation, that is purely subjective, indeed sentimental. Consequently, arbitrary individual choice becomes the sole law of love, which remains sunk in an intolerable but inevitable anarchy: we love arbitrarily, or rather, we believe that this arbitrariness still deserves the name *love*. We are thus reduced to the awkward paradox of being unaware of the logic and the rigor of that which we nonetheless continually acknowledge gives the sole flavor and meaning to our life. I love, I do not love, I am loved, I am not loved—without knowing why or, especially, what love is all about. Philosophy, which seemed in its Platonic impetus bound to allow movement beyond this aporia, seems, ever since it interpreted the world as what cognition cognizes exclusively, now to forbid it. Loving, like the rest (knowing, willing, desiring, being capable, and so on), amounts to representing (oneself). The fact that the master of representation has changed identity—*ego*, spirit, will to power—changes nothing with regard to its primal and unsurpassable idiocracy. What can I ever love outside of myself, given that the progress of loving consists in reducing all alterity to myself, under the figure of the represented? Emmanuel Lévinas takes up this aporia when he recognizes that "by an essential aspect love, which as transcendence goes unto the Other, throws us back this side of immanence itself: it designates a movement by which a being seeks that to which it was bound before even having taken the initiative of the search and despite the exteriority in which it finds it."[1]

However, when phenomenology introduces its new radicality by positing intentionality, does it not offer a way out of the aporia? We know, since and on account of Husserl, that "the basic character of intentionality" consists for consciousness in "the property of being a 'consciousness of something.' "[2] Consciousness characterizes itself by the strange, although trivialized, property of concerning first and above all what does not concern it. It is paradoxical, if one thinks about it, that we are not only conscious, but also conscious of something other than ourselves. It is one thing to notice that my consciousness never ceases to be affected with sensations, concepts, volitions, and the like; it is something else still more remarkable to notice that these "lived experiences of consciousness" *(vécus de conscience, Erlebnissen)* do not concern uniquely, nor even first, my consciousness, but objects transcendent and exterior to it, everything in it remaining immanent and so to speak coextensive. The lived experiences that weave the fabric of my consciousness nevertheless aim at an intentional object irreducible to my consciousness. Thus, in reading me, you experience experiences of consciousness (signs, already some fatigue, perplexities also, distractions, and so on). However, these lived experiences refer you to intentional objects that transcend your consciousness (the meaning of what I say, the very notion of

---

[1] Emmanuel Lévinas, *Totalité et infini: essai sur l'extériorité* (La Haye: Martinus Nijhoff, 1961), p. 232; *Totality and Infinity: An Essay on Exteriority*, tr. Alphonso Lingis (The Hague: Martinus Nijhoff Publishers, 1979), p. 254.

[2] Edmund Husserl, *Ideen I*, §36, Husserliana III (La Haye: Martinus Nijhoff, 1950), p. 81; *Ideas: General Introduction to Pure Phenomenology*, tr. W. R. Boyce Gibson (London: George Allen & Unwin, 1931 [1967]), p. 120.

intentionality that I am summarizing here, or else other notions that mobilize your attention, or other persons, and so forth). We think only intentionally because to think requires leading the lived experiences of our consciousness back to an intentional object other than my consciousness. To say that consciousness is consciousness of something means that it is not first consciousness of itself, but of something other than itself, that it is always outside itself—alienated, so to speak. The question, then, becomes quite clear: does not the intentionality thus sketched furnish the schema appropriate to a conceptual grasp of love, one that tears it away from the common interpretation? Wouldn't what phenomenology says about consciousness in general apply more exactly to love in particular, which would offer the privileged case of an intentional lived experience of consciousness, wholly "alienated" from itself in view of a prevailing intentional object, the other himself or herself that I love? And thus, wouldn't the path open directly toward the understanding of mercy? Let us see.

THE LIVED EXPERIENCE OF THE OTHER

Love counts indisputably among the states of consciousness. Beneath the figure of amorous passion, it even offers the most intense of all lived experiences of consciousness. If the expression "to fall in love" offers no precise meaning, at least it designates approximately the state of consciousness that Phaedra, standing before Hippolytus, stigmatizes definitively: "I saw his face, turned white! / My lost and dazzled eyes saw only night, / capricious burnings flickered through my bleak / abandoned flesh. I could not breathe or speak. / I faced my flaming executioner, / Aphrodite, my mother's murderer!"[3] For Phaedra, loving Hippolytus amounts to feeling certain lived experiences of her consciousness, imma-

---

[3] Racine, *Phèdre* I, 3, v. 273–277; *Phaedra and Figaro*, tr. Robert Lowell (New York: Farrar, Straus and Cudahy, 1961), pp. 24–25.

nent to it and as if indifferent to their supposed object. This indifference goes so far that Phaedra can thoroughly reveal these lived experiences of her consciousness to the one she loves by referring them, through an amorous ruse, to the one she ought to love, Theseus. Loving Hippolytus merges so much with the lived experiences of Phaedra, and so little with the actual singularity of the character Hippolytus, that Phaedra, inverting the same strategy of separation under the impulse of this alleged love, can accuse Hippolytus to Theseus and thus condemn him to death. What Phaedra loves is *not* Hippolytus, but the collection of lived experiences she feels under the name "Hippolytus," and that she moreover interprets lucidly as the effect within her, not so much of the real Hippolytus, as of divine vengeance (Venus). Accordingly, there is no contradiction in hating the very love that one feels in passion: this love does not consist in this or that person—who, from a distance, I could consider, help or curse—but in the collection of my own lived experiences of consciousness—immediately intermingled with my servile consciousness (*conscience serve* = *servo arbitrio*). The exceptional character of amorous passion is not an objection to this approach. All other love reproduces this characteristic: to love always means first to experience lived experiences of consciousness. Whether it is a question of kindness, friendship, or filial or parental care, I love only through the lived experiences of my consciousness. Even if I accomplish an altruistic duty without any sensible emotion, this absence of emotion already constitutes a lived experience of my consciousness. This analysis also must not be attenuated by the remark that love here only reproduces the universal characteristic of all knowledge—which, quite obviously, must pass through the lived experiences of my consciousness: everything that I perceive and comprehend, I experience first and finally in my consciousness, and not outside of it. Or, to speak like Descartes, "we know for certain that it is the soul which has sensory perceptions, and not the body."[4] For love

---

[4] Descartes, *Dioptrique* IV, in *Oeuvres philosophiques,* ed. Adam-Tannery [Paris: Vrin, 1906 [1966]) VI, pp. 6–7; *The Philosophical Writings of Descartes,* vol. 1, tr. John Cottingham, Robert Stoothoff, and Dugald Murdoch (Cambridge: Cambridge University Press, 1985), p. 164.

differs greatly from all perception; perception concerns only things or objects that I can, without their being contradicted, reconstitute, indeed constitute in and through myself; they can without any contradiction be thought as *my* objects; perhaps they even call for this on principle. But with love, it is a matter neither of objects nor of appropriation. In contrast, it is a matter of the other as such, irreducibly distinct and autonomous. If I were somehow to appropriate this other for myself, I would first have to reduce it to the rank of a slave, of an animal object, and thus lose it as other. Indeed, what explains the perception of the object—namely, its constitution in terms of the lived experiences of my consciousness—is the very thing that forbids love, for love should, by hypothesis, make me transcend my lived experiences and my consciousness in order to reach pure alterity. Whence the infernal paradox, universally suffered by all unfortunate loves as their definitive fatality: when I love, what I experience of the other, in the end, in reality arises from my consciousness alone; what I call love of another bears only on certain lived experiences of my consciousness, inexplicably provoked, in the best of cases, by a chance cause that I call the other, but that the other is not. Love appears as an optical illusion of my consciousness, which experiences only itself alone.

Amorous Autism

Let us confirm this quickly. What we might term the autism of love is marked by a paradox already formulated by Pascal[5]: I say that I love somebody, but I love her or him insofar as I experience him or her in my own conscious life as endowed with beauty, loyalty, intelligence, riches, power, affection for me, and the like. If certain, or all, of these lived experiences were to disappear, can I be certain that I would still love him or her? Let us suppose the best of cases: I would continue to love this other without his present beauty, his present intelligence, and so forth; in short, apart from all the glamour that

---

[5] *Pensées* §323/688.

my conscious experiences record; in this (highly unlikely) case, I cannot continue to say that I love her for herself, because I no longer have at hand any lived experience of consciousness to permit me to identify her. In fact, even if I love in spite of a withering abstraction from all lived experience and every accidental quality, I simply no longer know *who* I love; properly speaking, I am loving in the void. And this paradox does not concern only the sickly nostalgia of Madame Bovary; it concerns the limit cases of therapeutic relentlessness, where the technique no longer offers anything to love but the abstract of all conscious experience, thus the abstract of the other. Love is identified with the lived experiences of my consciousness, not by an excess of my egoism that a bit of altruism might offset, but by a law of my consciousness; the other cannot appear to me, even to be loved, except through the lived experiences of my consciousness—it is not a matter of morality, but of phenomenology. Thus when I experience love, even a sincere love, for the other, I first experience not the other but my lived conscious experience. Supposing, then, that I still love another than myself, at the very least, I love him *in* me.

At a deeper level, the autism of love belongs to the domain of self-idolatry.[6] For there remains an objection to our analysis: if I love the other in me, I still love the real other, because I do not love just anyone or everyone, but this and that one, this or that one. I love an identifiable, individualized alterity, thus foreign to myself. Even if Proust's Swann could love a woman who was not of his type, he loved her alone, Odette, and not some other, Madame Verdurin or Oriane. But why, exactly, will what I call *my* love invest this particular figure? Because this figure arouses the most powerful, rich, and abiding lived experiences in my consciousness; that is, this figure fills my desire and my capacity for experiencing, to the point that all the lived experiences issuing from other figures or from the inanimate world are, by comparison, im-

---

[6] Baudelaire, *Fusées* XI, in *Oeuvres Complètes*, "Pléiade," ed. Y.-G. Le Dantec and Claude Pichois (Paris: Pléiade, 1966), p. 1,256.

mediately disqualified and as if immaterial. If this figure imposes itself on me, the reason is found less in it, unknown anyway, than in me; I experience in it the maximum of lived experiences that my consciousness tolerates and calls for. Love fills my consciousness because it takes the measurements of my consciousness and submits itself to that measure. Confronted with what I name the other, I see not her but the sum of lived experiences, for which she is only the accidental cause and of which my consciousness is the real measure. In short, if I love this and not that other, it is because the first reflects more exactly the measure of my desire for lived experiences, and therefore of my consciousness. My love is mine only inasmuch as it is for me *less* other than every other love, only insofar as it fills my consciousness with lived experiences, because in fact it reflects my consciousness. I must, then, name this love *my* love, since it would not fascinate me as my idol if, first, it did not render to me, like an unseen mirror, the image of myself. If I love *in* myself the other, it will therefore be necessary that I love *myself* in the other—that I love in the so-called other only the idol of myself. Love, loved for itself, inevitably ends as self-love, in the phenomenological figure of self-idolatry. My love always amounts to the love of myself. In other words, because in this love I love myself, I thus love concretely only those who love me. Whence the judgment of Christ: "If you love those who love you, what reward do you deserve? Do not the tax-collectors do as much? And if you hail only your brethren, what have you done that is so special? Do not the gentiles do as much?" (Matthew 5:46–47). If we stick to the definition of love as a fabric woven from the lived experiences of my consciousness, we turn all love back upon ourselves, with a reciprocity that poses no difficulty, because it lacks exteriority. According to the unique presupposition that love plays itself out in my conscious experience and gives me the perfect idol of myself, it attracts what it loves to my consciousness, like the sun attracts the planets, like hatred attracts hatred—necessarily.

The Other, the Aim, and the Object

This paradox marks an impasse, and this impasse results from a unilateral choice: we have used only one of the two terms in the doctrine of intentionality—the lived experience of consciousness. Yet, our concern is precisely with the term that does *not* imply intentionality as such. Intentionality is not identified with the lived experiences of consciousness, but on the contrary identifies them with what they are not— with the intentional object. Intentionality does not have as its object the immanence of lived experiences, but the transcendent object; it aims, through these lived experiences, and by polarizing them toward itself, at the objective of the intentional object. Intentionality renders consciousness intentional of something other than its own lived experiences, namely the object itself. The very fact that the intention most often oversteps intuitive fulfillment confirms the fact that consciousness aims at more than it lives, thus that it aims at an object that is definitively other than itself. Consciousness, by and with its polarized lived experiences, becomes always consciousness of an other, consciousness altered by alterity itself, intrinsically alienated consciousness. Hence, just as the interpretation of love on the basis of the immanence of lived experiences to consciousness brought to light the self-idolatry of passion, its interpretation on the basis of the transcendence of the intentional object should lead to the thought of its authentic alterity. Or, to cite Husserl: "What I demonstrate to myself harmoniously as 'someone else' and therefore have given to me, by necessity and not by choice, as an actuality to be acknowledged, is *eo ipso* the existing Other for me in the transcendental attitude *(der seiende Andere)*: the alter ego demonstrated *(ausgewiesen)* precisely within the experiencing intentionality of my ego. . . . 'In' myself *(in mir)* I experience and know the Other; in me he becomes constituted—appresentively mirrored *(appräsentativ gespiegelt)*, not constituted as the original."[7] The ambiguity of

---

[7] *Cartesianische Meditationen* §62, Husserliana I, p. 175; *Cartesian Meditations: An Introduction to Phenomenology,* tr. Dorion Cairns (Dordecht: Kluwer, 1995), pp. 148–149.

Husserl's thesis is exposed unambiguously: the other is reached only at the end of an intentionality that, however radical it might be, remains no less the intentionality in and of my consciousness. Alterity completes intentionality, without transgressing it or putting it into question—in such a way that the ego confirms the absolute phenomenological primacy of the "region consciousness," and thus of itself. The other arises as constituted by the ego. Such a constitution of the other can certainly illustrate one of the dimensions of love: namely, that love consists precisely in a dimension that intentionality opens, untiringly decentering the immanence of consciousness and distending without limit its lived experiences, in view of a vanishing point that is by definition always beyond what any intuition will reach. Intentionality implies the never resorbed surplus of intention over intuition, of the object aimed at over its fulfillment, of the dimension over its crossing. Thus it becomes definitively clear that the other, which my love claims to love, will always have to transcend my consciousness by overstepping it, like the horizon whose line recedes in proportion as one draws near to it. The intentional object is not an object, erected after the fact into the object of an intention; on the contrary, it is an intention that gives rise to an objective, without ever doing so adequately and without remaining an object. This point once established nevertheless immediately compels an investigation: the intentional object, if it remains a tangential objective more than a totally constituted object, is no less the objective of the always original ego, of the constitutive *I* that my intentionality assumes. This presupposed condition inflicts on principle a subordination on what it conditions; the fact that the object results from the intention nevertheless does not deliver it from the condition of being conditioned; the fact that it always remains tangentially unknown does not free it from having to depend on an intention awaiting fulfillment. The intentionality of consciousness submits objects, and nothing but objects, to consciousness, as to an *I*. Now, by definition, we are seeking access, via love, to a subject, and thus precisely not to an object—

however distant he may be. Intentionality opens only onto
the objectivity of intentional objects, and never directly to
another subject: in the field of the aim, only one origin, one
intentionality, one *I* can be at play. To suppose my intentional aim at the other to be followed by intuition, and thus
by success, would for that very reason fail, because intuition
can fulfill only an intention toward an object. Every success
of intentionality would reach, exclusively, an object, and
would thus fail to encounter the other as such. If the imper-
fection of its fulfillment qualifies intentionality and so instructs
us in alterity in general, its eventual success disqualifies it
from instructing us in the subjectivity of the other. The intentionality of consciousness indeed opens consciousness infinitely, but opens it only to the horizon of objects, and thus
closes it radically to the encounter with the other subject,
with the other as subject, with the other as such.

The Invisible Gaze

The request to think the other as subject offers all the ambiguities of the very term "subject." The reversal of perspective—of perspective itself—will therefore have to be
accomplished, if it can be, without recourse to the "subject,"
to its aporiae and its potentialities. One must give up seeing
the other as a subject, and for a radical reason. The other
must remain invisible so as to offer himself to a possible love,
because if, by chance, I saw him (if an intuition adequately
fulfilled the intentional objective, a hypothesis that is highly
debatable for every legitimate object), he would be ipso facto
already disqualified as other. As soon as Orpheus wants *to see*
Eurydice, he transforms her into an object and thereby disqualifies her as beloved. He makes her disappear because he
does not admit her as invisible. Only the object is visible, and
the entrance into visibility qualifies an object as such. The
object alone has to be seen, not the other. Why, then, would
the other not have to be seen? Because nothing can be seen
which does not first have to be intended, and nothing can

be intended except as an objective submitted in advance to
the gaze that constructs its object. What renders the other
decidedly other than me, and first of all other than all the
objects wherein I ceaselessly accomplish myself, stems not
from a certain quality of its objectivity—but from this: the
other is characterized in that she too intends objectives, she
too constitutes objects, she too precedes a world. I carry out
the function of a transcendental *I* only insofar as I intend objectives, which can thus become visible objects, and inversely, can neither intend me nor see me. If someone other
than me—precisely, *the* other—accedes to the function of *I*,
he must by hypothesis exert an intention that renders visible
the objectified objectives and therefore render himself invisible. The intention, which incites the visible, cannot itself be
seen. If the other deserves this title, he necessarily will have
to enter into invisibility. The other, as other, irreducible to
my intention, but origin of another intention, can never be
seen, by definition. This paradox is confirmed in the immediate experience of the exchanged gaze. If I want truly to
gaze on the other, I attach myself neither to her silhouette,
however pleasing it might be, nor to some voluntary or in
voluntary sign that her bearing might reveal, but to her face;
I face up to her *(je l'envisage)*. "Facing up" to her does not
mean fixing my gaze on her mouth or some other emblematic element but fixing exclusively on her eyes, and directly
in their center—this ever black point, for it is in fact a question of a simple hole, the pupil. Even for a gaze aiming objectively, the pupil remains a living refutation of objectivity,
an irremediable denial of the object; here, for the first time,
in the very midst of the visible, there is nothing to see, except an invisible and untargetable *(invisable)*[8] void. When
"faced up to," the center of the eyes does not shy away, because it does not sustain my gaze; even if this face does not
turn away, it hides, in its petrified immobility, within its pupils, the visibility of every possible objective. In not shying

---

[8] [Translator's note: the French *invisable* signifies "that at which one cannot aim" *(viser,* "to target," "to aim at").]

away from my gaze, the gaze faced up to or envisaged itself hides the very horizon of the visible. How does it succeed in doing this? Or, which amounts to the same question, why do I insist in gazing on what hides all objects from me?

AGAINST THE CURRENT OF CONSCIOUSNESS

A single response no doubt suits both questions. Of the face offered to my gaze I envisage only what cannot be seen in it—the double void of its pupils, this void that fills the least empty gazes imaginable—because if there is nothing to see *there*, it is *from there* that the other takes the initiative to see (me). Gazing on the other as such, my eyes in the black of his own, does not imply encountering another object, but experiencing the other of the object. My gaze, for the first time, sees an invisible gaze that sees it. I do not accede to the other by seeing more, better, or otherwise, but by renouncing mastery over the visible so as to see objects within it, and thus by letting myself be glimpsed by a gaze which sees me without my seeing it—a gaze which, invisibly and beyond my aims *(invisablement)*, silently swallows me up and submerges me, whether I know it or not, whether or not I want it to do so. The gaze of the other, or better, alterity as gaze, is not "hypertrophied consciousness, but consciousness that flows against the current, overturning the consciousness" (E. Lévinas).[9] Consciousness that flows against the current, indeed the counter-current of consciousness: the other does not become accessible by means of intentional consciousness, but at the price of consciousness's very intentionality.

---

[9] "Un Dieu Homme?"In "Qui est Jesus-Christ?" *Recherches et Debats* 62 (1968): 186–192, reprinted in *Entre nous: essais sur le penser-à-l'autre* (Paris: Editions Grasset & Fasquelle, 1991), pp. 69–76. See "La trace de l'autre," in *Tijdschrift voor Filosofie* (1963, no. 3), reprinted in *En découvrant l'existence avec Husserl et Heidegger* (Paris: J. Vrin, 1988), p. 195: "Consciousness loses its primary place. . . . The visitation consists in upsetting the very egoism of the I, the face unseats the intentionality that aims at it. At issue here is the putting into question of the consciousness, and not a consciousness of the putting into question."

Consciousness, *my* consciousness, should not claim to reach the alterity of the other by diving into its own depths as an intentional consciousness; for intentionality merely radicalizes the irreducible and solitary primacy of the gaze of a subject on its objects. In short, with the best intentionality in the world, consciousness can intend and see only objects, thus forbidding itself the alterity of the other. The other remains invisible to my consciousness, not despite intentionality, but because of it. The alterity of the other transgresses, even and especially, the intentionality of *my* consciousness from the moment that consciousness reverts all the more to me as mine in its spreading out ever more intentionally from me. I never accede to the other on the basis of the consciousness I have of him, but always in opposition to this sudden consciousness (of him by me). I do not reach the other by means of the consciousness I have of him; he forces himself upon me by means of the unconsciousness to which he reduces my consciousness. Of the other, who slips away as visible object, I can only passively experience the invisibility—losing consciousness of him. The other, or my loss of consciousness. But if the very movement wherein my consciousness exteriorizes itself confirms the imperially self-enclosed primacy of my consciousness, that is, if my opening still belongs to me, as the horizon where the sun of my power never sets, is it necessary, if we are to have any hope of loving, to enter into a twilight of all consciousness, to expose ourselves in all unconsciousness to the black sun of an invisible light?

I Is Not Just Anybody[10]

That the other is imposed on me in and through the unconsciousness to which he reduces my consciousness, destitute

---

[10] [Translator's note: The French title of this section is "*Je* n'est pas le premier venu." *Le premier venu* means, literally, "the first to arrive"; when used with a negative in a sentence like that of the title, however, it means "X is not just anybody." Both meanings are played upon here and throughout the section as a way to argue, against Lévinas, that the other is always a particular other, "not just anybody" but always "just such" a particular other *(un tel).*]

of intentionality, supposes a paradox: the invisible gaze of the other can actually reach me, in an irreducible exteriority. In order to think through this, it behooves us first to establish the nature of the exteriority here at issue. In the phenomenological attitude as well as in the natural attitude, exteriority only opens out from an originary pole, whose interiority is fixed in the *I*. Intentionality does not modify this presupposition, seeing as it always implies the difference between a "here" and a "there" and the flesh of my body can only inhabit a "here." In all cases, I remain an *I*, who defines exteriority on the basis of interiority, transcendence on the basis of immanence, what is intended on the basis of its denominating—and thus dominating—intentional aim. For an invisible gaze to impose its intentional aim on me, it is necessary that the *I* discover itself preceded by a causal authority that certifies its own primacy in dismissing that of the *I*. It is necessary that the denominating domination yield to an uncontrollable anteriority, that of a primary exteriority. Exteriority can, in effect, result not from the interiority of the *I*, but rather destabilize it, precede it, and not proceed from it. For exteriority to be emancipated from the interiority that defines the *I*, it is necessary that it disqualify the denominative power of the *I*. The *I* can falter only if, far from naming the poles of exteriority as its objects (objectives of its intentional aim), it itself finds that it is the object of another aim, in short only if the nominative *I* dismisses itself in the accusative *me*. Of the forever invisible other, of whom I can never say that I see him as such (precisely because it is *I* who sees), I know at least that he aims at *me*, as the objective of his invisible intentional aim. His gaze brings out the features of the *I* to the point where no traces remain of it other than a simple and naked *me*. Literally, *I disclose myself*; or more explicitly: the other strips bare the *I* within me to the point of leaving only the *me* exposed. The *I* discloses itself before another gaze and discovers that only a *me* remains. The *me* designates the *I* uncovered, stripped bare, decentered. *I* become me by uncovering myself as the simple *me* of an other; *me* indicates not what the gaze of the other aims at and shows (which is said by a *you*), but what the already evanescent *I* experiences of the gaze of an other trained upon it, or better, what the *I* experiences of himself as evanescent beneath the gaze of an other. I become me by discovering myself as the faltering shadow of *I* in the denominating gaze of the other—who came first. The other, hereafter not just anybody *(le premier venu)*, says *I* and fixes me as the direct complement, an objective, of his invisible, exterior and first aim.

The Injunction

This reversal can be made less abstract. Exteriority happens as its most intimate determination to the one who discovers himself in the accusative: if not accused, at least put into question and brought to trial by an anterior injunction. Without any exterior voice compelling me, the injunction brings me to discover myself as obliged by another: I must devote *myself* to . . . it is incumbent upon *me* to . . . this or that, he or she obligates *me* to. . . . I do not read on the other's face the direct visibility of the other in person (and thus an objectivity which, strictly speaking, would be deposited only in a cadaver), but rather my own summons to lay myself open to him. To lay oneself open or expose oneself to the other means first, outside all visible sensibility, to experience ethical responsibility for the other. If I never rejoin him directly, he always enjoins me, indisputably. He makes his invisible gaze felt and weigh upon me by letting the nonsubjective and nonmasterable feeling of respect be born within me. I know and feel, as if in spite of myself, that I am responsible for the fate and the death of my brother. Thus the obligation—which makes itself felt in the feeling of responsibility, inasmuch as the responsibility exceeds the responses that, in the irrepressible feeling of my guilt, are brought by me—summons me in advance before the tribunal of the other. Before being conscious of myself *(Selbstbewusstsein)*, I am conscious of my obligation, thus of my fault *(Gewissen)*, vis-à-vis the other—the first come *(premier venu)*, who makes me the last of the last. The injunction renders me responsible *for* the other (Lévinas) and not simply *in front of* the other (Sartre). Even if the other did not see me and thus could not judge me, I would experience, by discovering *me* myself as an accusative dismissed of the nominative, that I owe *myself* to him: in order for him to live, I owe it to him to dedicate myself. I do not measure his right over me by what my existence can, once affirmed, concede him. I experience that my existence will undergo the injunction of the first to arrive and will overdetermine self-consciousness by a bad consciousness (of self), exactly proportionate to the consciousness of the (unfilled) obligation to the other. I lose consciousness of myself because I am conscious of my obligation to the other before and more than I am conscious of myself. Remorse delivers to *me* the sole consciousness of myself, which will not perish, because it delivers the *I* unreservedly, already destroyed before being, to the invisible and silent injunction of the other, whose fate comes down to *me*. The rights of the *I* collapse beneath the infinite obligations that come down to *me*. I can never say anything to the other except my shortcomings and my belatedness. But it is these very things that open me to him by detaching me from the intentionality of the *I*.

THE CROSSING OF THE GAZES

The unconsciousness that we are seeking can therefore be reached. It is not a matter of an unconsciousness wherein the process of a likely love is clouded over with illusory ambiguities; nor is it a matter of simple inversion of the axis of the gaze, where the function of the *I* simply displaces itself from one to the other of the terms at play, thereby reinforcing all the more its validity. Instead, it is a matter of a consciousness that exerts itself on my consciousness, without following it into polarization in terms of the *I*—a consciousness against the grain of the *I*. The moral injunction *(Gewissen)* brings to bear the consciousness of an obligation that imposes itself on the *I* and thus destroys it as originary pole. Still, consciousness is not closed up *(Bewusstsein)* in the indistinctness of the id. The *I* reduced to the *me* retains consciousness, precisely so as to see that it no longer becomes conscious of *itself*, but of an obligation that links it, despite itself, to the anterior other. The moral consciousness forbids the transcendental consciousness to fold itself back over and into an *I* and enjoins it to see itself as consciousness, in itself, of the other than self. The moral consciousness contradicts self-consciousness by counterbalancing the intentionality exerted by the *I*, thanks to the injunction summoning *me*. The injunction constrains and contains intentionality; intentionality objectifies the other on the basis of the *I*, but all the same, the injunction summons *me* on the basis and in the name of the invisible other. The invisibility passes from one extreme to the other, the means alone remaining visible to the corresponding aim. Whence comes what we will from now on consider the phenomenological determination of love: two definitively invisible gazes (intentionality and the injunction) cross one another, and thus together trace a cross that is invisible to every gaze other than theirs alone. Each of the two gazes renounces seeing visibly the other gaze—the object alone can be seen, the eye's corpse—in order to expose its own invisible intention to the invisible impact of the other intention. Two gazes, definitively invisible, cross and, in this crossing, renounce their invisibility. They consent to let themselves be seen without seeing and invert the original disposition of every (de)nominative gaze—to see without being seen. To love would thus be defined as seeing the definitively invisible aim of my gaze nonetheless exposed by the aim of another invisible gaze; the two gazes, invisible forever, expose themselves each to the other in the crossing of their reciprocal aims. Loving no longer consists trivially in seeing or in being seen, nor in desiring or inciting desire, but in experiencing the crossing of the gazes within, first, the crossing of aims.

LIVED EXPERIENCE CROSSED

Determining love as the crossing of aims gives rise to a clear-cut difficulty: does the crossing itself remain invisible or does it rise to visibility? Put another way, does it become an object, which can actually be seen as a lived experience of consciousness? We will try to argue that the crossing of the invisible gazes becomes visible only for the parties involved, because they alone undergo an experience without recognizing an object in that experience. The intentional gaze, if it crosses the moral injunction, experiences an interdiction, an obligation, or a provocation. It matters little whether it respects them or transgresses them, for in both cases this intentional gaze will actually feel the weight of a counter-aim, a weight that is all the more objective in that, in order to pass beyond, the intentional gaze will require the imbalance of a higher weighing—which would thus be more highly actual. The ethical counter-aim makes its weight felt with the same force whether I transgress it or subscribe to it, whether I resist it or consent to it. But if gazes that are foreign to one another see nothing of the crossing of two invisible gazes, in short if this nonobjective crossing remains decidedly invisible to them, too, things are not the same for each of the two concerned gazes—the two gazes concerned each by the other. The intentionality of the *I* and the obligation to the other (which opposes *me* to him) cross, in that they experience each other; they experience each other in the common lived experience of their two efforts, constrained each to the other, buttressed by their contradictory and thus convergent impetuses. Intentionality and the injunction exchange nothing, especially not two (objectified) lived experiences; yet they come together in a lived experience which can only be experienced in common, since it consists in the balanced resistance of two intentional impetuses. This common lived experience results from the crossed conflict of two invisibles: without one, without the other, without both the one and the other in strict equality, the lived experience either would not be fixed or else would not remain in a lasting equilibrium. The two gazes are balanced in a common lived experience, which does not touch them in their respective origins, but summons them and finally blocks them in their mutual impetuses, to the point of balance in their crossing. With the two invisible aims, this crossing traces a cross, still invisible except to those who suffer its weight in a common lived experience. Thus, in crossing swords, duelists experience something like a single lived experience that communicates a common tension—the pressure that my weapon, and thus my arm, and thus my whole body imposes, contains, and renders to the opposed pressure. Whence I infer an arm outstretched and an entire fighting body, which exerts against me the intention that I exert against it. Arm wrestling, where the two arms cross and where the impetuses of each of the two bodies are immobilized, brings together, face-to-face, the two fleshly faces. What then do each of these two invisibles see of the other? Nothing objective, nor visible (the two adversaries still remain nondead, nonvisible because not cadavers). However, they see their encounter, for they experience the weight of each impetus one against the other, a unique and common weight, balanced and shared. They see, with their always invisible gazes, the lived experience of their tensions. The crossing of gazes here imitates the crossing of swords—what they each see of the other consists in the balanced tension of aims, like two weapons crossed. The crossed encounter is made to stand as a lived experience of the invisible; however, the experienced vision of the lived experience never results in the visibility of an object. The crossing of invisible gazes draws near to being quasi-visible only for the two aims that experience, like a heavy weight falling on the shoulders all at once, the balance of their two impetuses buttressed at full force. Neither the lover nor the beloved encounter each other in passing, dreamily, each in the other. They experience one another in the commonality of the lived experience of their unique tension—the weight of one gaze on the other, crushed by experiencing itself seen, crushing by seeing itself experienced. Two gazes, which seek each other, seek not the invisible site of the other gaze, but the point of equilibrium between my tension and his or her own. The sudden fixity of their common level, like water equilibrated in a lock, does not arouse in them any less inexpressible pleasure than bodily pleasure. For bodily pleasure, perhaps, comes down to generalizing for all flesh the balance of aims, where each attests to its humanity by honoring itself with invisibility—as if with glory. Whence the inverse consequence, that pleasure can answer to the high name of love only as a common lived experience, where two invisibles balance each other; if they fail, the pleasure sinks into insignificance, or, if it claims to overcome insignificance, it sets itself up as an unforgivable posturing as the invisible—an obscene incarnation of the gazes' corpse. The pleasure of the eyes disfigures the pleasure of the gazes, wherein no object— especially not a heart or a face—can bring climax, for climax *(la jouissance)* is born from the inobjectivity that only the tension of the gazes governs. A visible jubilation of invisibles, without any visible object, yet in balance, through the crossing of aims: let this situation count, here, as the sketch of a definition of love.

ORIGINARY ALTERITY

To define love as the crossed lived experience of invisible gazes implies, at the very least, that the gaze of the other reaches me and weighs upon my own gaze. We have admitted under the name injunction the advent of a gaze other than that of my own intentionality. The injunction benefits from a noteworthy privilege: it is a lived experience of mine in that it greatly affects my consciousness; I experience the obligation that imposes itself on me and compels me, whether I admit it or not; the obligation affects me directly, inevitably, to the point that I cannot release myself from it by handing it off to someone else, nor even make him experience it (except if he directly experiences a parallel obligation). For the injunction is not received by derived appresentation, in which the originary presence would reside in the other. The injunction does not enjoin the other to me simply because it might come from him; it does not result from a disposition of the other, wherein it would reside first and actually, so as then to pass from an originary presence to a derived presence. The injunction does not come from the other toward me, by an inverted intentionality of the other consciousness acting against my own. It actually arises in me, as one of my lived experiences, which an originary presence assures to my consciousness; yet, as a lived experience of my consciousness, the injunction imposes on my consciousness, without the least bit of intentionality (neither its own, nor another's), the first coming of the other. From the beginning, I experience the rights of the other over me, as more original to me than myself. The injunction makes another gaze weigh on my own, another gaze of which the other knows nothing and, literally, of which he has no idea. In the best of cases, the physical gaze of the other furnishes only the schema of the injunction; or rather, I can regard the other as an invisible gaze (and not see him as an object) only because first of all the injunction imposes him on me, designates him to me and leads me to him—despite myself, but also despite him. The injunction does not come to me from the other, nor does it push me toward him: it makes me experience, in and through myself, the advent of the other; I experience myself, in myself and as such, obliged to an other who can be entirely ignorant of this obligation. The obligation toward the other is born in me, though it is not born of me; it is born for him, though it is not born through him. The obligation, really and truly mine, makes the original weight of a gaze that the other does not even have to produce weigh upon me; or rather, the invisible gaze of the other can come to bear on my own gaze only to the degree that the injunction in me precedes it and welcomes it—contrary to all intentionality.

THE MEANS OF THE UNIVERSAL

The privilege and the paradox of the injunction alone make possible a phenomenological sketch of love. But in this di-

rection a difficulty also appears: the injunction certainly incites me toward the other, but without my having to or
being able to discern love there. If the injunction enjoins to
any other whatsoever, indeed to every possible other, simply
inasmuch as it offers the face of man, it does not permit the
election of such an one, precisely because it enjoins rendering to the other as other what I owe him. The injunction
gives rise not so much to love as to duty, for, like duty, the
injunction concerns every other, universally. The injunction
addresses me to the other in order that I offer him the recognition that he deserves as end, and not as means, or, which
amounts to the same thing, the continuation of the particular
maxim guiding my action into the universality of a law. The
formal universality that determines my behavior toward the
other does not in any way depend on the particular identity
of this or that other. The formal universality of the obligation
becomes thinkable only once persons have been abstracted
from it, such that the other opened by the injunction can be
played by anyone: the other thus passes from one face to the
other, according to the radical substitution that universality
imposes. That the particular face here holds the role of the
other, without incarnating him definitively, that this face occasionally lends its gaze to the universal injunction, in short
that this other remains only the lieutenant of the other *(l'autrui)*, finds its confirmation in respect. Without a doubt, the
injunction of the law moves me to respect, whether I transgress it or obey it, and thus becomes as particular as my sensibility. But it is precisely this respect, which I experience in
particularity, that I do not feel for *this* other, *this* face, *this*
individual, but rather for the universal law alone. My individuality submits to affection for the universal, and never for
the other who accidentally lends his face to it. Far from my
individuality feeling for another, individually unsubstitutable
by the mediation of respect for the universal of the law, my
individuality instead lets itself be moved by the accidental
and substitutable mediation of any individual face in favor of
the universal of the law (to the point of becoming, like a free
noumenon, itself universal). Accordingly, and paradoxically,

the moral law—which states that the other man must always count as end and not as means—never uses the face of an individualized other except as a means for accomplishing the universal. The injunction of obligation toward the other *(autrui)* leads, in reality, to the neutralization of the other as such. The other is neutralized as other, for another can always be substituted who can offer the face of the other *(d'autrui)* that the universal moral law requires: no face can claim to be irreplaceable because, if it in fact became so, at once, by right, the act accomplished in regard to him would cease to satisfy the universality of the law. The other as such therefore undergoes a second neutralization: to the substitution that is, on principle, always possible, there is added the always required gap between the law and *every* singular individual. Between the letters of the law all possible individuals can and must parade, with equal dignity—which is to say, without any dignity, except borrowed, lent by the law itself. The injunction does not lead to loving *this* other, if only the universality of the law pronounces it; rather, it leads to the law itself, while neutralizing the other in particular *(comme un tel)*.

THAT FACE

The injunction therefore must be singularized for my gaze to cross an individually irreducible gaze. It attains this singularization in passing from obligation to responsibility: "It is my responsibility before a face looking at me as absolutely foreign . . . that constitutes the original fact of fraternity."[11] Responsibility inverts the legal arrangement of end and means: I am responsible not in front of the law by means of the other, but directly for the other by means of the injunction itself; the death of the other, or his life, depend directly on my regard for his open face; the other unreservedly constitutes the sole stake of my responsibility; nothing surpasses

---

[11] Lévinas, *Totalité et infini,* p. 189; tr. Lingis, p. 214.

him, surprises him, or utilizes him. The suspicion of neutralization does not disappear, however. For I am responsible standing before every other, provided that his face exposes itself to my gaze; and it is precisely this provision that enables substitution to remain possible: each of the visible faces enjoins upon me a responsibility which at once prompts and orients my own intention; in order to compel my responsibility, a face suffices, every face, each face, indeed, any face, so long as it opens in an invisible gaze. The unconditioned nature of responsibility implies its universality, from face to face, up until the last, whoever that might be. The neutrality persists because a substitution persists. To be sure, the Neuter, *here*, owes nothing to the Neuter that Lévinas stigmatizes in the primacy of the ontological difference; it is not a question of neutralizing the face, nor a being, nor being in its variance with Being; but the face itself neutralizes unsubstitutable individuality; I do not find myself responsible before *such an one* as much as *this such an one* admits of being reduced to *a* face in general, addressee of my gaze, and conjuring of its aim. Now, recourse to a face in general leaves two difficulties unbroached: (1) Where will things stand with the disfigured face? No doubt, it is in just such an undone face *(un tel visage défait)* that the essence of every face must be squarely faced. It nonetheless remains the case that to approach this disfiguration as to a face, one needs to employ a gaze that recognizes and knows how to envisage; not every gaze, even those already affected by responsibility, succeeds. What gap, then, separates the recognition of the disfigured face from its nonrecognition? Responsibility, doubtless, is not enough, not excluding its eventual and explicit deepening. (2) Can the other, designated to me by a face, individualize himself to the point of becoming unsubstitutable for every other other? This question opens out into another question: Why am I enjoined by this other and not that one? And if the reason for this should not be sought, we must then acknowledge that the injunction concerns alterity in its universality, as indifferent as possible to *such* or *such*. No doubt, ethical responsibility cannot, and even must not make distinctions between faces, such that, *with regard to responsibility,* the universality of the injunction implies no return whatsoever of the Neuter. But, if we are seeking to define love as it is distinguished from respect and responsibility, then the possibility of substituting one face for the other constitutes a final obstacle, all the more fearsome because it results directly from love's most advanced approach.

THAT TO WHICH I ENJOIN MYSELF

In order to bring love back to its conceptual determination, we were obliged to subtract it from representation, even intentional representation, so as to substitute for it the injunction. The injunction itself now remains to be determined, so that it will not settle into any figure of the Neuter. If we want to secure responsibility all the way to the point of love, then the injunction must designate not only the other as such, but *just such* an other as the invisible gaze that crosses my own. That *just such* an other enjoins me implies that he sets himself up as unsubstitutable and strictly irreplaceable. Not only would "The other . . . no longer be now, where I respond for him, the first-come *(le premier venu)*—he would be an old acquaintance,"[12] but he would also no longer be something known at all, if science bears only on the universal, or at least on the repeatable. The other as *such* redoubles his invisibility with a particularity unknowable in itself. Love passes beyond responsibility only if the injunction reaches atomic particularity: love requires nothing less than *haecceitas,* which is also situated beyond essence (unless we must say on the hither side of essence). *Haecceitas* passes beyond beingness *(l'étantité)* in general, but also beyond that which, in the injunction and responsibility, falls under the universal, and thus

---

[12] Emmanuel Lévinas, *De Dieu qui vient à l'idée* (Paris: J. Vrin, 1982), p. 250; *Of God Who Comes to Mind,* tr. Bettina Bergo (Stanford: Stanford University Press, 1998), p. 166. It could even be that the other, neither known nor replaceable, belongs, more than to the past and the present, to the future—no matter what happens, the other will always be just such *(tel).*

the Neuter. It pierces all the way through to the unique, which no fellow will ever be able to approach, nor replace. The other as such asserts itself as the other of all the others, and does not reside in itself alone except insofar as it separates from everyone else. *Haecceitas* decides for an absolute separation from every similitude, to the point of provoking the holiness of the other. The other alone singles out himself.

Such a claim immediately gives rise to an objection. Does the singular particularity of the other as *just such* an other—as the sole and unique one—not reproduce, displaced from the one (the I) to the other (the other as such), the fundamental injustice of every self: to insist upon oneself as a basis, which, under the heading of irreplaceable center, centralizes the world into so many interests, to the point of including, as if these interests were reducible to the Same, men to whom this self denies any face? Does not the other win its *haecceitas* as an ultimate and full proprietorship that appropriates the other, starting with my own gaze, which he claims from me with injunction? In short, does not *haecceitas*, as unsubstitutable center and appropriating proprietorship, repeat what Emmanuel Lévinas denounced as "mineness," the characteristic of *Dasein* that disqualifies it ethically? This characteristic of the self appropriating itself to itself in the experience of its nonsubstitutability—the egoity of *Dasein*[13]—reappears in the injunction of the other as such, since the *as such* is fulfilled finally (and ever since Leibniz)[14] only in the *I*. The other as

---

[13] Criticism (for example in *De Dieu qui vient à l'idée*, pp. 81–83, 145–148) of Heidegger, *Sein und Zeit*, §9: "The Being of this entity is *in each case mine*. This entity, in its Being, comports itself toward its Being. As entity of this Being, it is delivered over to its own Being. Being is that which is an issue for this entity each time" (*Being and Time*, tr. Macquarrie and Robinson [New York: Harper & Row, 1962], p.67 [translation modified]). *Jemeinigkeit* compels *Dasein* to personalize with a pronoun the verb to be only on the basis of its radical claim *(Anspruch)* by Being. Whence Lévinas's attempt to institute a claim prior to that of Being (*De Dieu,* p. 245, 265; see *Le Temps et l'autre*, 2d ed. [Montpelier: Fata Morgana, 1979], p. 133 ff.).

[14] "Because it is necessarily the case that in corporeal nature we find true unities, without which there would be absolutely no multitudes nor collection, it must be that that which makes corporeal substance would be

such would only open onto an *alter ego*, an alterity still under the figure of the *ego*, and thus an alterity reduced to the Same: this other amounts to the same as me, since we both come back to the figure of the *I*. An *I* displaced still remains an *I*, radically foreign to all alterity as such. And to accede to such an other, simply a displaced *I*, neither love nor ethics would be required—a simple knowledge through analogical appresentation of one monadic ego by another would be enough. In claiming to pass beyond ethics through love, we would only have regressed to ordinary intentionality of consciousness. The objection, however, is less forceful than it appears: it proceeds as if the unsubstitutable other could be understood as a displaced *I*; or more precisely, as if a displaced *I* still remained, rightfully, an *I*; and therefore as if the unsubstitutable character of the other (what makes him *just such* this other) could be reduced to the egoity of the *I*. But of course a capital difference opposes them: I impose my egoity (or impose myself through it), while the unsubstitutability of the other is not imposed on me by him, but indeed by I who seek it as such (or seek him as *just such* within that unsubstitutability). The other requires his *haecceitas* not because he imposes it on me as his rule, but because *it is necessary for me* that it be imposed in order that the injunction allow me to experience his gaze as such. Inversely, I can and even must renounce my own, my proprietorship of egoity, for the sake of exposing myself to alterity; but I cannot—for

---

something which responds to that which I call the self [*moy*] in us, which is indivisible and yet acting" (G. W. Leibniz, *Système nouveau pour expliquer la nature des substances* . . . , in *Die philosophischen Schriften*, ed. Gerhardt, IV, p. 473). As a result, on the basis of the I, and without ever contesting it, every other other can be reached: "The reflexive acts, which enable us to think of that which is called *I* . . . and it is thus that in thinking of ourselves we think of Being, of Substance, of the simple and compound, of the immaterial, and of God himself" (*Monadologie*, §30; *G. W. Leibniz's Monodology: An Edition for Students*, ed. Nicholas Rescher [Pittsburgh: University of Pittsburgh Press, 1991], p. 21). Whence the perfect diagnosis offered by Nietzsche (14 [79]): "We have borrowed the concept of unity from our 'I' concept—our oldest article of faith" (Nietzsche, *Werke,* ed. Colli and Montinari [Berlin: Walter de Gruyter, 1972], vol. III/3, p. 50; *The Will to Power*, tr. Walter Kaufmann [New York: Viking Press, 1962], p. 338).

that very reason—renounce proprietorship, what is proper to the other, if I want to encounter the injunction of his gaze as such. *Haecceitas* does not reproduce, as a symmetrical reply, the egoity of an *I*; it reverses it. The other resolves himself in the crossing of gazes on the condition of entering this crossing as unsubstitutable, while I enter it only on condition of leaving myself destitute of all intentionality, and thus of all egoity. What is more, intentionality directly contradicts unsubstitutable particularity, because it has as its unique function to permit consciousness to substitute itself for every thing; consciousness is intentionally every thing, thus it itself is counted among none of these things; the unreality of consciousness results from its intentionality and dispenses it from identifying itself among things. *Haecceitas* thus marks the renunciation of intentionality and egoity, and thus stigmatizes the precise act by which the other enters into play as *such*—namely as stranger to an *I*. The injunction that would finally put into play the other as such would, thus, also accomplish the transgression of intentionality by love.

The Invisible Unsubstitutable

But a conditional will weaken this confirmation, as long as we have not established that an injunction actually imposes upon me the gaze of the other as *such*. Can such confirmation ever emerge? Perhaps, if one considers further the injunction itself. (1) The injunction asserts itself upon my gaze because it weighs upon it with the weight of another gaze. Why does this gaze itself weigh in with all of its weight? Because the other in person exposes himself to it. Why then does he lay himself open to it to the point of imposing on me? Because, as we have just seen, the other only becomes absolutely "just such" an other *(tel)* by becoming unsubstitutable for every other other. The other accedes to himself by coming forward in his irreplaceable *haecceitas*; he is thrown off balance, so to speak, by jumping into his alterity with a step that throws him into the final singularity. The other poses his gaze as inescapable injunction only insofar as he weighs into it with all his weight; and he weighs with all the weight of alterity only insofar as he throws himself madly into his alterity. But *haecceitas* is not accomplished as such (does not reach the end of its individuality) unless the other as such becomes unreservedly ecstatic. Now ecstasy, understood in the sense of the Aristotelian ecstasy of time, is summed up in the gaze, which weighs with the weight of *haecceitas* only insofar as *haecceitas* surpasses itself and comes to die in the gaze, as though in a final impetus. The alterity of the other as *such* attains its final individuality because it moves ecstatically, through its *haecceitas*, into a gaze: the other passes completely into his gaze, and will never have a more complete manifestation. Whence a twofold consequence: finally, only the gaze can be called unsubstitutable, and this gaze is simply one with the injunction, since the injunction enjoins for the sake of the other as such. (2) If the injunction that I receive gives me, in a gaze, the last possible ecstasy of the other, it delivers the other to me, without remainder, without reserve or defense, the perfect operative of the unsubstitutable in him. The injunction thus enjoins me to support, with my own gaze, the unsubstitutable alterity of the gaze of the other as such. To support a gaze means to support the invisible unsubstitutable within it. That it can only be an invisible gaze is newly confirmed in the impossibility of an unsubstitutable objectivity—the object is seen, is defined, and is therefore repeatable. The unsubstitutable is fulfilled only in a gaze (ceaselessly other), because it is the operative of alterity itself. The gaze wherein the other is exposed as such can, in weighing on my own, only enjoin him to expose himself in turn to unsubstitutable individuality. The gaze that accomplishes in itself the unsubstitutable can only enjoin me to accomplish, in projecting myself within a gaze, my unsubstitutable. If in his gaze the other risks himself in his last individuality, he can only enjoin me to risk myself, in return, in my ultimate individuality—to risk rendering the unsubstitutable to the unsubstitutable. Note that it is not a matter of reestablishing two self-possessors, and thus two *I*'s.

Rather, it is up to each one to let himself be summoned, by another's injunction, to his own individuality, entirely completed in the ecstasy of the gaze—not for the purpose of retaking possession of self by reintegrating what is proper to him, but in order to expose himself in person to the final ecstasy of the other. I owe the other for making me, under his absolutely unsubstitutable gaze to the point of nakedness, also unsubstitutable, individualized, and naked. The other's exposition enjoins me to expose myself, too, in order to shelter it, to maintain it, and to protect it. I receive my unsubstitutable individuality from the advance of the other in his gaze; I receive myself, then, unsubstitutable from his own ecstasy. I receive it as *such* because it provokes me to make myself an *as such*. The injunction imposes upon me the gaze of the other *as such*, since it imposes upon me to expose myself there, in person, as *such*, by myself moving ecstatically into my unsubstitutable gaze. The other comes upon me as such, because he renders me indispensable—the injunction exerts itself as a summons.

Freed from intentionality,[15] love in the end would be defined, still within the field of phenomenology, as the act of a gaze that renders itself back to another gaze in a common unsubstitutability. To render oneself back to a gaze means,

---

[15] Lévinas's critique of intentionality admits different degrees; sometimes, it is only a question of freeing intentionality from the pair subject/object (*En découvrant l'existence,* p. 139) or from the couple noesis/noema (*Totalité et infini,* p. 271); other times, it is more radically a question of attaining "a non-intentional thought whose devotion can be translated by no preposition in our language—not even the *to* which we use" (*De Dieu,* p. 250, see pp. 184, 243, 261; *Of God Who Comes to Mind,* tr. Bergo, modified, p.166). No doubt, today, its author would no longer subscribe completely to the thematization that he gave of love in terms of intentionality: "The act of love has a sense. . . . The characteristic of the loved object is precisely to be given in a *love intention,* an intention which is irreducible to a purely theoretical representation" (*La théorie de l'intuition dans la phénoménologie de Husserl* [Paris: Alcan, 1930], p. 75; *The Theory of Intuition in Husserl's Phenomenology,* tr. André Orianne [Evanston: Northwestern University Press, 1973], pp. 44–45); the meaning of the act of love (if it is still a matter of an act) exempts love not only from "purely theoretical representation," but even more from every intention, because from all intentionality.

for another gaze, to return there, as to a place for a rendez-vous, but above all to render oneself there in an uncondi-tional surrender: to render oneself to the unsubstitutable other, as to a summons to my own unsubstitutability—no other than me will be able to play the other that the other requires, no other gaze than my own must respond to the ecstasy of *this particular* other exposed in his gaze.

But to render oneself other, to surrender this gaze to the gaze of the other who crosses me, requires faith.

July 1983

5

The Crucial Crisis

A Crisis of "Crisis"

Two THINGS, and doubtless hardly more, are averred about what it is convenient to call "the crisis": first, that we do not know how to resolve it, and, next, that in all likelihood we do not know how to define it. Or rather, as soon as it is a question of evoking it, we break it down into an infinity of "crises" that are obviously not decisive by virtue of their very accumulation. For conservative minds, the issue becomes a "crisis of values;" for progressives, a "crisis of economic growth"[1] or a crisis of adaptation (to new technologies, to the *new deal* of the global economy), in short, a transitional crisis; sociologists will speak of a social crisis, economists will distinguish between crises in energy, in natural resources, and in the international monetary system. And, if one prefers to speak in the grand style, one could even go so far as to invoke and analyze a crisis of western civilization as such, resulting from a crisis of the "man" whom it has constructed and upon whom, in turn, it rests. We have neither the desire nor the competence to attempt such a classification of these acceptations of the term "crisis" according to their respective relevance. We are simply noting an obvious fact; the multiplication of occurrences implies the devaluation of the concept; if we possessed a precise concept of crisis, and if we could apply it rigorously to the present situation, it would integrate a majority of these aspects, today dispersed and merely juxtaposed. It is therefore necessary to suppose a crisis of the concept of "crisis," before sup-

---

[1] Jean-Paul II, "Message au peuple français, 27 May 1980," *Documentation Catholique* 788 (15 June 1980), p. 551.

posing any social crisis or crisis of our age. Unless the purported crisis in our society and our time locates itself precisely in the crisis of the very notion of "crisis."

Can one outline a notion of "crisis?" Even without entering into the etymology and the medical occurrences of the term, it appears that "crisis" implies decision and judgment. But this decision after judgment would not present any urgency or any stakes if it remained abstract. The crisis arises only at the conclusion of an analysis of the antagonisms that provoke it; if these antagonisms concern the exchange of goods, the crisis will be economic—thus Marx: "The general possibility of crises inheres in the formal metamorphosis of capital itself, in the temporal and spatial non-coincidence of buying and selling."[2] The crisis does not consist merely in deciding, but in determining the mismatch between supply and demand, and thus supposes an analysis; without this, there will only be a "potential crisis,"[3] and thus, in fact, no crisis at all. Accidental difficulties are not enough to set the crisis in motion; proof lies in the unconscious resolution of crises that the bourgeoisie achieves in economics without analyzing their "ultimate reason"[4]; without this analysis, bourgeois society "prepares more extensive and more destructive crises, by diminishing the means whereby crises are prevented."[5] As long as the terms of the conflict and the rationality which necessarily opposes these terms are ignored, it makes sense not to speak of a crisis: the crisis begins, on the contrary, with the rational understanding of the conflict. Consequently, in classical tragedy, the crisis culminates, before any decision, in the lucid consideration of the conflict and its unsurpassable, because necessary, antagonisms. What better example than, in Corneille's *Cinna,* the long mono-

---

[2] Karl Marx, *Matériaux pour "L'Economie"* in *Oeuvres, Economie II,* vol. 2, tr. Maximilien Rubel (Paris: Pléiade, 1968), p. 480.

[3] Marx, *Matériaux,* p. 478.

[4] Karl Marx, *Capital: A Critique of Political Economy,* vol. 3, tr. David Fernbach (New York: Vintage, 1981), p. 615.

[5] Karl Marx and Friedrich Engels, *The Communist Manifesto,* in Robert C. Tucker, ed., *The Marx-Engels Reader* (New York: W. W. Norton, 1978), p. 478 (translation modified).

logue by Augustus, who has just learned of his friend's final betrayal? It is power itself that appears unbearable—"Take back the power you have endowed me with, / If with more subjects it brings fewer friends" (IV. 2. 123–124). But this contradiction results inevitably, first from the crimes committed by Octavius in order to become Augustus (1,129–1,148), and next from the republican tradition of Rome (1,149–1,179); so that, as a result, only three hypotheses are possible: kill the traitor, commit suicide, or kill the traitor *and* commit suicide. That at the end of this analysis, Augustus has still not decided—"Which of the two to follow in my pain? / Ah, let me die, or tell me I must reign" (1,191–1,192)—does not prohibit speaking of a crisis, since the conflict has already received its perfect analysis.[6] The solution subsequently chosen—unconditional clemency—will be possible only by a radical passage beyond all the hypotheses retained by the monologue (as is often the case in Corneille); in effect, the resolution of the crisis implies the analysis of the competing claims and their irrefragable necessity only insofar as it transgresses them by the affirmation of absolute freedom and, therefore, without sufficient reason. The decision does not follow from the analysis—otherwise there would not be a decision, but a simple consequence; the decision transcends the analysis and settles it once and for all. But, for that very reason, the decision assumes the analysis. A last component is still missing, alongside decision and analysis of conflicts: the very possibility that a decision might resolve the necessary antagonism of the contradictory forces. This is not a mere platitude; often, the eventual decisions do not settle the conflict, but merely betray the panic and feeling of impotence at not being able to settle them. The decision either masks the crisis through ignorance of the conflict, or hides the busy incapacity to resolve it. An authentic crisis thus supposes the almost miraculous conjunction of an analysis and a will; it implies that the choice of an individual or a

---

[6] Pierre Corneille, *Seven Plays,* tr. Samuel Solomon (New York: Random House, 1969), pp. 245, 247.

group can also count as the theoretical solution to a necessary conflict.[7] Here it is not a matter of considering as a crisis only a conflict already resolved by a decision, but, rather, of stating more precisely that one can speak of a crisis only if the possibility remains open that a free decision offers its solution. After all, a natural catastrophe, a world war, an international economic confrontation, and so on do not constitute a crisis for individuals, but merely a fatality to be borne; while, in contrast, a sickness, a professional challenge, a human encounter, and so forth can provoke a crisis because they admit into the mix the decision of a free will. To speak of an economic or a political crisis is meaningful only insofar as, within a democracy and a liberal economy, each individual, as citizen or economic agent, participates in decisions that are nonetheless global or collective. If all these modes of participation ceased to function, it would no longer be necessary to speak of a crisis, but simply of unfavorable states of fact. In this sense, when the victims cannot make an effective decision for resolving the conflict, it becomes illegitimate to speak of a crisis, and still more of individual responsibility. In short, we understand by crisis, a conflictual situation analyzed as necessary, such that it is at least possible that a free decision could resolve it.

NEUTRAL HISTORY

We can return to the investigation we began with—the crisis of "crisis." I will argue the claim that we, today in France, and therefore in one of the few liberal democracies still in existence and in one of the hardly less rare developed economies, that we are not in a state of crisis. In other words, I will take up, though for other reasons, the paradox advanced by Alain Minc, "We are entering the time of the after-crisis, because there has not been a crisis."[8]

---

[7] Among other examples of a concluded political crisis, note Charles de Gaulle, *Mémoires d'espoir,* vol. 1 (Paris: Plon, 1970), chap. 1.

[8] Alain Minc, *L'après-crise est commencé* (Paris: Gallimard, 1982), p. 7.

(1) There has not been a crisis because the terms of the conflict are not known. Or more exactly, in each conflict, hypotheses can be supported with a strange and new indifference. In economics, the (authentic) crisis of 1929 offered two opposed options, clearly contradictory and therefore equally falsifiable: liberalism and social democracy; the latter prevailed in all countries (including the fascist). Today, though, it is perfectly possible to analyze the reigning stagflation as a failing of social democracy as well as a failure of liberalism (monetarism, etc.). Politically, too, one is free to interpret the slowdowns in contrary terms: we suffer from "too much State," or else we suffer from economic anarchy and stateless businesses; the fact that politicians explain that these formulae remain compatible can only heighten the astonished distress of the ordinary citizen. The international tension can be analyzed as a reinforcement of bloc politics just as well as an uncontrolled atomization of local conflicts, such that the concept of "international crisis" no longer applies today as it did in 1905, in 1913–14, or in 1939. World population, however unregulated it may be, does not furnish us with the example of a crisis: it can just as well be analyzed as a (local) overpopulation as the consequence of aborted economic "take-offs"; inversely, the rampant underpopulation of developed countries proves that economic growth can provoke the inverse of what it nonetheless renders materially possible: the "welfare" of a large population. The examples could obviously be multiplied. Let it suffice to emphasize their common lesson: a crisis becomes possible only if constant, identifiable, rational antagonisms sustain it; a mismatch observed but still incomprehensible to models and concepts does not make a crisis; the very accumulation of pretended crises, entangled and always displaced, attests that we quite simply do not understand these conflicts, and can in no way succeed in reducing this accumulation to a single theory. Gathered information and discordant alarms are not enough to draw up a diagnosis; for a diagnosis supposes an etiology and every etiology implies a science. There has been no crisis, not because difficulties have been lacking, but be-

cause their identification fails to appear. We have not entered into a crisis, except blindly and through failure to understand. Certain struggles have been or soon will be won (for example the energy "crisis," the inflation "crisis," and so on); but these struggles have concerned only the induced effects of a challenge that itself remained unknown; these victories resolve no authentic crisis; on the contrary, they exacerbate the uncomfortable feeling of not even having understood what or who must be fought. Whence the tormenting certainty, ill hidden by the official discourses, that the worst is still to come—the anonymous worst. There has not yet been a crisis because we lack the understanding of it.

(2) To speak of a crisis, we still need a decision, which can actually be made. But who today could decide? No doubt an indefinite number of economic, political, military, and cultural agents never cease making "official" decisions. But these decisions concern only a particular order, and however powerfully they might be carried out, can only confine themselves there. The most powerful multinational company in the world, the most enormous of imperial powers in the world, the most widely diffused of networks in the world can give (or take) only what they have (or strive after); their initiatives remain subject to the iron-clad laws, partially unknown, that predetermine their reciprocal games. In all cases, these deciding powers can only claim to dominate, unchecked and unlimited, simply to satisfy the incoercible necessity of their growth. Now we all know that the game will be decided in terms of self-limitation (of arms, of birth rates, of genetic manipulation, of production, of standardization, etc.). Thus the more the decision-makers decide, the more they further the misunderstanding of the question. The more they decide for the increase of their power, the more they show themselves to be decidedly "decided" by the logic of power, rather than the "deciders" of the terms of the debate. The impossibility of the decision, and thus of the crisis, is also marked quite clearly at the other extreme of the chain of power. The free choice of individuals can decide nothing here; no doubt because each individual has available only a

very limited effective power, no doubt because individuals lack information; but above all, the impossibility to decide results first and foremost from a feeling of irresponsibility. By dint of hearing it repeated that "we are all responsible for everything that happens in the world," we have understood that the inverse alone must be true: it is *not* I, as an individual, who am responsible for malnourishment, drought, unequal distribution of wealth, so-called wars of liberation, terrorism, and totalitarianism, and so forth. This responsibility is *not* directly mine, and for a very simple reason: my concrete, actual, and measurable decisions, in short what depends on my free choice, which remains the "only thing in us which could give us good reason for esteeming ourselves,"[9] in no way influence, at least not directly, these permanent and structural evils. And if I am responsible, it is first of all for my neighbor: a task that is sufficient to exhaust my attention and my spontaneous altruism. If one puts forth counter-examples (commitment to humanitarian associations, aid to the underdeveloped world, solidarity with Solidarity, and the like), one must at once note an essential difference: the personal decision becomes actual in these cases, because the responsibility there is real. And it becomes so only because the everyday networks of the macro-structures are bypassed, suspected, disqualified; in short, because other analyses, other parameters, and other agents are found mobilized, this time freely; here it is the unpredictable freedom of individuals that incites, rather than results from, the analysis, the structures, and the decisions. In this very particular context, decision once again becomes possible. But it is clear that at this time this inversion is still marginal, except in certain privileged and exemplary cases: civil society in Poland, the ecclesial communities in Africa and South America, and perhaps the intellectual community in Western Europe. The macro-structures remain incapable of decisions, and the

---

[9] René Descartes, *Passions de l'âme*, §152; *The Philosophical Writings of Descartes*, vol. 1, tr. John Cottingham, Robert Stoothoff, and Dugald Murdoch (Cambridge: Cambridge University Press, 1985), p. 384.

decision-makers remain fundamentally the "decided." There has not yet been a crisis because we lack the possibility and the courage to decide.

(3) If its two constitutive elements are missing, it is therefore not legitimate to speak of a crisis. We are living a semblance of crisis, which endures only as long as appearances do not enter into a real crisis: the appearances of decision, the appearances of an analysis of the opposed antagonisms. Thus we continue to pretend to know the stakes, in order to continue to be able to pretend to make decisions. This double, or rather too simple, game lets its inadequacy stand out in the sadly famous formula "crisis management." Obviously, a crisis is not managed; it is understood and decided. A doctor standing before his patient, like Augustus confronted with Cinna's betrayal, does not manage; he analyzes and then acts on the problem. "Crisis management" amounts to admitting—which counts more than dissembling[10]—that we lack either the knowledge of the rational necessity at play or the free decision, or, probably, both. Whence the present situation, characterized by indifference. In philosophy, indifference affects freedom when the will does not have at its disposal an evidence of the understanding to guide it; here the indifference results not only from the absence of evidence, but from the absence of decision; it is a case of indifference to power. We therefore suffer less from a crisis than from an absence of identifiable and decidable crisis; in other words, our crisis is born on the second level of an undecidable state, of a state in crisis at not being a state of crisis. It is not only because there has not been a crisis that we are not entering into the after-crisis; we have entered into crisis because no crisis has arisen, which would permit a global understanding of the origin of the mismatches and allow for clear decision-making. It is not only because there has not been a crisis that we are not entering into the after-

---

[10] The dissimulation of the crisis often uses the formula "aggravation/ deepening of the crisis" to stigmatize its adversary. A still quite current, exceptionally pertinent example can be found in Georges Marchais, Le défi démocratique (Paris: Grasset, 1973), particularly pp. 7–9.

crisis: we are in crisis precisely because the mismatches are mounting without coming to a crisis. For ten years (in the short term), or for a century (in the long term, and according to Nietzsche)[11] we have remained in the pre-crisis—and it is this very fact that places us in a state of crisis. *State* of crisis: the formula is self-contradictory, since crisis marks precisely the moment and the means of a transition. But *our* crisis consists exactly in that the crisis is forever awaited, the decision is not made, the antagonisms endure—an incessantly postponed and forgotten waiting.

My Death

The current acceptations of "crisis" therefore merely make manifest the deficiencies of the determinations of the concept of crisis that lie within them. Neither economics, nor politics, nor sociology can today present an object that satisfies the conditions of possibility of an authentic crisis. Without a clearly analyzed antagonism, the decision does not decide but instead remains a symptom, itself decided, of the obscure necessity; we must renounce the hope for *the* final crisis as thematized by Nietzsche: "The *value* of *such a crisis* is that it *purifies* . . . from the point of view of health, it gives a start to a hierarchy of forces."[12] In our history, the end of crisis succeeds the myth of the final crisis.

In our history—but which one? All our analyses of a possible crisis have, until now, admitted as evidence its historical frame, or rather have interpreted history as collective and universal. But in fact history, except when confined to the formal object of historical science, comes from *my* history

---

[11] Friedrich Nietzsche: "What I relate is the history of the next two centuries. I describe what is coming, what can no longer come differently: *the advent of nihilism.*" Fragment 11 [411] in Nietzsche, *Werke,* ed. Colli and Montinari (Berlin: Walter de Gruyter, 1970), vol. VIII/2, p. 421; *The Will to Power,* tr. Walter Kaufmann and R. J. Hollingdale (New York: Vintage, 1968), p. 3.

[12] Friedrich Nietzsche, Fragment 5 [71], *Werke,* ed. Colli and Montinari, vol. VIII/1, S.221.

and is reducible to it. Even if, by means of studies and com-munications, I manage to assume, for a moment, the point of view of Sirius, I still remain within history because my life, decidedly finite, shares for only a short time the course of the supposedly universal and neutral history. The first and, finally, the sole history that I know and can accomplish is my own contingent, limited, mortal history. All history amounts to my history, because it derives from it. There is no solip-sism in this circle, just the admission that my life remains mine, unsubstitutable, unique, unrepeatable—thrown forth and lost at once. Why does history itself amount to *my* his-tory and my history to irrevocable uniqueness? Because I must die. To die signifies to die alone. To die signifies that nobody will die in my place; the proof: if someone commits himself to die in my place, that will not exempt me from dying, later, on my own account, and, if it can be put thus, in my own place; there is no one but me who can truly die in my place; my place is even defined by this unsubstitutable death. Death will never be taken from us, and in the end it is death that attests our irreducible singularity. No one can separate me or dislodge me from my death, for in order to take it from me he would have to begin by giving it to me. In this death, which makes me *me* at the very moment when it undoes my *me*, all is decided for and by me, and all the former antagonisms are settled. We must say, then, that one crisis remains accessible to me when all the others have lost their edge and slipped away—my death.

All the "crises" of macro-history, whether they fail to stand out clearly (as today), or whether they are perhaps ac-complished (as in the past), remain in any case attenuated re-flections and imprecise anticipations of the sole crisis effectively possible because necessarily actual—my death. My death as the sole certain event of my life, once my life has been born; for once my life has been born, I am assured only of its end. We do not have to sketch here an analytic of my death, for others have already brilliantly succeeded in doing so. We have only to insist on one point: death would not necessarily break in as my death, nor as the ultimate horizon of my possibility, if it did not befall me as the crisis par excellence. Death determines me as (my) Being-for-death only insofar as it determines me, that is to say imposes itself upon me as my ultimate crisis.

WHAT MY DEATH DOES NOT DECIDE

If death imposes itself as the first and the last crisis, it should be possible to show that it satisfies the three determinations of a crisis.

(1) Death completes a known antagonism, or at least one experienced as such. It might be health slowly eaten away by sickness or degeneration; more profoundly, it might be the struggle between the will-to-live and the will-to-disappear; it might be, finally, the conflict between self-conserving egotism *(conatus in sua esse perseverandi)* and the unreserved gift of self. In every case, an agony unfolds, and thus, properly speaking, a combat, which the ultimate blow decides only by exacerbating it. Every death, and not just that of John the Baptist, is "Like a clean rupture / That serves to dissever / The ancient disharmonies"; and not only the disharmonies "With the body,"[13] but also and above all those of the mind with itself. For the final antagonism that death confronts consists after all in death itself, which signals the maximum contradiction by designating itself as "the characterized possibility of the impossibility of existence" (Heidegger).[14] Death announces itself as the inescapable horizon, therefore also as the highest possibility of life; but what it announces, in announcing itself as possibility, is called (the) radical impossibility (of life); in short, it is not so much that death confronts an antagonism as it *is* this antagonism itself—

---

[13] Stéphane Mallarmé, "Le Cantique de Saint Jean," in *Oeuvres Complètes* (Paris: Pléiade, 1945), p. 70; *Collected Poems,* tr. Henry Weinfield (Berkeley: University of California Press, 1994), p. 49.

[14] Martin Heidegger, *Sein und Zeit* (Tübingen: Max Niemeyer Verlag, 1967), p. 306; *Being and Time,* tr. J. Macquarrie and E. Robinson (New York: Harper & Row, 1962), p. 354.

the possibility of impossibility from which comes the impossibility of possibility.

(2) Death decides this antagonism that it is. By a new contradiction, it itself annuls the contradiction that it constitutes. In the end and in all cases, I die and this death decides all by ending all. This decision alone removes the contradictions by its own contradiction. And here, precisely, it is not a paradox that only a paradox undoes a paradox, but rather an absolute necessity. This ultimate hour reveals the truth of all the preceding ones by summing them up more than by annulling them: "Again it is the first; / And it is still the only one, —or it is the only moment."[15] The absolute in this decision stems from the fact that, no matter what happens, I not only must but also can die; no conflictual situation will hem me in to the point of forbidding me the freedom to decide its antagonism by death; it is not necessarily or first of all a matter of suicide, but most often of flight forward, of risk run, indeed of sacrifice of self for others, in short of the surging advent of the future. My death can always decide the crisis of my life. Inversely, my life remains undecided so long as death has not decided it. So long as Oedipus has not reached the crisis of death, no one can say to him, even when witnessing the most glittering prosperity, whether or not his life is (or was) happy: "Then learn that mortal man must always look to his ending, / And none can be called happy until that day when he carries / His happiness down to the grave in peace" (Sophocles).[16] Reciprocally, on the eve of a victory, Solzhenitsyn concluded: "Call no day happy until it is done; call no man happy till he is dead."[17] Death not only ties the Gordian knot of life, but cuts it, too.

(3) A final characteristic of the crisis remains: that the deci-

---

[15] Gérard de Nerval, "Artémis," Les Chimères, in Oeuvres, ed. H. Lemaître, vol. 1 (Paris: Garnier Frères, 1958), p. 702.

[16] Sophocles, Oedipus Rex, v. 1528–1530; tr. E. F. Watling, The Theban Plays (London: Penguin, 1947), p. 68.

[17] Aleksandr Solzhenitsyn, The Oak and the Calf: Sketches of Literary Life in the Soviet Union, tr. Harry Willetts (New York: Harper & Row, 1979), p. 186. See the commentary offered by Corinne Marion, Qui a peur de Soljénitsyne? (Paris: Fayard, 1980).

sion that settles the antagonism of the conflict really belongs to me. On this point the nevertheless privileged crisis of death offers, at least if one sticks to its purely natural and so to speak "pagan" meaning, a paradoxical insufficiency. Of course, I alone die, and, without possible substitution, must live my death. And of course, only death will work out the truth of my life, which it will decide for the first and last time. However, at the moment when *I* die and when *my* death is decided, I am neither the witness nor the fashioner of this very decision. In holding to this world—by methodological hypothesis or by "pagan" conviction—without admitting any other after it, I must conclude that I will never know the decision that I allow death to make about me. It is I who die, but it is not I who see the decision thus made about my life. At the instant when I die, and therefore when my truth is decided, I am for the first time no longer there to contemplate it. Someone will say and will know whether I was a liar or loyal, a magnet or a lover *(un aimant ou un amant)*, a thinker or a buffoon, a swindler or a worker, and so forth—*someone*, that is to say everyone and no one, each and every anybody, every possible man, my friends and my enemies, my neighbors or strangers, but in any case not me. Death plays itself out in me and puts me into play as my first crisis; but it decides about me without me. This judgment, the first to work out the truth about me and my contradictions, escapes me at the very moment it embraces me. The truth slips away from me in the very act in which it overtakes me. The crisis is perfectly accomplished in everyone's eyes, except mine. When I finally become present to public truth, I am not around to see it. In short the mortal crisis judges me only in absentia. The crisis that comes to me with my death steals from me my judgment. Never will I know my truth, which everyone else nevertheless will know. Then again, will they know it? Won't indifference, prejudices, passions, and forgetfulness, occurring nonintermittently or at best every few hours, obfuscate the judgment? And further, is it not necessary to admit that there will have been a crisis only for me? A crisis without judgment, neither for me who is already absent, nor for the others who are indifferent to every other crisis but their own—this is really quite natural. Death thus draws near to being a crisis. But, by definition, it ultimately cannot confer upon me the property of a crisis, because it consists precisely in disappropriating me of myself. The crisis of death cannot go so far as to become an authentically final judgment. Death passes beyond all other sketches of crises, but without attaining or even suggesting the final judgment. So, I seek an authentic crisis only in the hope, no doubt rather insane, of a judgment which, in the last instance, judges me, and wherein I know what I am and what I am doing. Death cuts me off too soon to give me the crisis. It provokes the hope for a crisis, which it takes away from me. Like Tantalus, the more I see it draw near, the more I know that it will steal the crisis from me. The absurdity of death lies not in the putting to death of my life, but in its frustration of meaning, not in the execution of judgment, but in the silence of any judgment. We die—there is nothing unjust or absurd in that. But we die without knowing the truth. We die absurdly because we die of a crisis without any last judgment. Death, or the unfinished crisis, purgatory awaiting a judgment; for the "worst punishment of purgatory is being uncertain about judgment" (Pascal).[18]

THE INVERTED JUDGMENT

We are seeking a completed, finished crisis, a crisis where the antagonism finds a decision that works out the truth about me, but also for me and with me. We are seeking a crisis that is completed because driven all the way to the truth. Thus, because the truth about me would contradict itself if it did not manifest itself to me and was decided without me, we are seeking a crisis consistent with my freedom—a free crisis. A free crisis implies, according to what was established earlier, at the least a free death. We should therefore resume the

---

[18] Pascal, *Pensées*, §518/921.

search starting from the hypothesis of a free death. Free was the death of he who could say: "For this reason the Father loves me, because I lay down my life, that I may take it again. No one takes it from me, but I lay it down of my own accord. I have power to lay it down, and I have power to take it again; this charge I have received from my Father" (John 10:17–18). Jesus Christ has the power (ἐξουσία) to give his life—literally to lay it down, to expose it, like a victim in the desert, like a wager placed on the gaming table— precisely because he also has the power to take it up again. But he gives it in an almighty freedom for the sake of submitting himself, the first and preeminent, to the paradoxical mystery that he comes to reveal: "He who loves his life loses it, and he who hates his life in this world will keep it for eternal life" (John 12:25). The question concerning the free crisis henceforth becomes: Can Christ, absolutely free at the edge of the crisis of death, which for us remains incomplete, introduce us into a completed crisis, that is to say into a crisis of, for, and through our freedom?

The passion and the death of Christ accomplish "the crisis of this world" (John 12:31): the world finds itself judged by this crisis; that we may (and should) translate κρίσις by "crisis" as well as by "judgment" means that, in the "right κρίσις" (John 7:24 = 5:30) and in the "truthful κρίσις" (John 8:16 = Revelation 16:7), the crisis comes to completion by delivering an explicit and in the end public judgment on the world. Before suggesting a condemnation (as in John 5:24–29), the κρίσις accomplishes the crisis by means of a judgment, the very judgment which, until now, was missing from the so-called crises. By its duplication in the shape of a judgment, the crisis becomes at last and for the first time crucial. However, the crucial character of the crisis does not reside in the ambivalence of the word κρίσις, a simple semantic given of the Greek in general. The ambivalence of this term appears *here* only insofar as an actual and unique event makes it flagrant. What event? It would seem theologically correct to answer: the death of Christ provokes a crucial crisis because in it God judges the world, counts his own, announces and already realizes the last judgment; and for that matter, exegesis has made it exceedingly clear that the stories of the Passion consciously adopt the traditional elements of eschatological discourse. These pieces of evidence are indisputable. But it remains that the crisis becomes, in the death of Christ, crucial only insofar as it is, quite to the contrary, the Christ who undergoes therein "the judgment of death, κρίμα θανάτου" (Luke 24:20) on the part of men. The crucial crisis does *not* arise from a judgment of Christ: "God sent the Son into the world, not to judge (κρίνῃ) the world, but to save the world through him" (John 3:17), "If any one hears my sayings and does not keep them, I do not judge him; for I did not come to judge the world, but to save the world" (John 12:47). Christ is forever refusing to exercise judgment and to institute the crisis by condemning sinners, as men demand of him; even on the cross, he prays the Father to spare his own executioners from judgment (Luke 23:34). And in fact, the Father himself precedes the Christ in this refusal to execute the crucial judgment that would condemn: "The Father judges no one" (John 5:22). Neither the Father nor the Son judge men. On the contrary, it is men who judge Christ and, in him, their Brother, by grieving the Spirit: "Pilate said to them, 'Take him yourselves, and judge him (κρίνατε) by the crisis that your own law permits' " (John 18:31).[19] The previous interrogations of Christ by the scribes and the priests, like the outrages and the mockery to come, fall under this scandalous but unquestionable paradox: in the crisis between men and God, man always claims the role of judge, the judgment is always the death sentence, and the condemned always God. All men, even the most holy, have accused God. It is even by this that

---

[19] One thinks here of John 19:13, which, according to Ignace de la Potterie, reports that Pilate made Jesus sit on the *bêma* in the position of judge, *pro tribunali*, before designating him as such to the Jews: "Behold your king!" Accordingly, Jesus appears at once as judge and judged, and men condemn themselves by the simple fact that they do not admit that he is the only true judge: he judges them inasmuch as he is judged unworthy of being judge, "he is their judge because they refuse that he should be their king" ("Jésus roi et juge d'après *Jn* 19, 13," *Biblica* 41 [1960]: 217–247).

one recognizes a man—by his condemnation of God: the modern "atheists" copy not only Adam and Cain, but also Job, Moses, Peter and the others. Such inversion of the crisis judgment, besides its intrinsic scandal, forbids elaboration of a finally completed crisis: the free crisis is reduced to a wicked judgment made by men, and awaiting repeal.

SELF-JUDGMENT

Nevertheless, this paradox does not take away our access to a completed crisis; rather, considered more closely, it in fact opens that access to us, definitively. If God does not judge and if men alone judge, the crisis nonetheless reaches its completion, for men, in unjustly judging God, judge themselves with all justice in relation to God. The crisis draws to its perfection not because God would judge, but because Christ, in deserting the role of judge and abandoning it to men to the point of risking his own death, provokes men to judge themselves with full knowledge of the case: each becomes his own judge according to the decision he makes in the crisis, which Christ provokes in the pure announcement of the words of his Father. For Christ has neither the right nor the need to judge; he has only the duty to propose to men the crisis that God himself considers completed—the unsurpassable revelation of God himself. Standing before this word laid bare, each man enters into crisis: either he refuses it in order to die (in the guise of living) by himself, or he accepts it in order to live (in the guise of dying) by the Spirit of God poured into his heart (Romans 5:5). Christ does not judge, he provokes the completed and unsurpassable crisis, by the word that the Father delivered to him—the crisis in which each man must decide about God for himself, and thus decide about himself facing God. "This is the κρίσις: the light has come into the world, and men loved darkness rather than the light" (John 3:19; see Romans 1:21–22). The crisis is not brought about because a strange judge appears before powerless man, but because, in meeting the ultimate

word, each man enters into his own crisis—and must, on his
own, decide himself for or against "the word of God . . .
piercing to the division of soul and spirit, of joints and mar-
row, to judge (κριτικός) the thoughts and feelings of the
heart" (Hebrews 4:12). The crisis is constituted so to speak
as a third term between God and men: God does not judge,
nor does his Christ; he decides nothing, but offers men the
conditions for their highest decision; the neutral judgment
that Job absurdly calls for is granted by God: he provokes the
free and completed crisis of man by freely delivering to him
an absolute word in the face of which all truth is made, as far
as concerns what man truly wants. Man will in the end be
able to decide for himself by himself, according to the perfect
freedom that only the Perfect and the Free can give. "If any
one hears my sayings and does not keep them, I do not judge
him; for I did not come to judge the world, but to save the
world" (John 12:47): thus, though man's rejection of his sayings would rightfully merit a condemnation, Christ decides
that the crisis rightfully will not happen. Should we infer
from this that, after having assembled the conditions for the
crucial crisis, Christ suspends its course? Not at all: he merely
remands it to the full freedom of man himself: "He who rejects me and does not receive my sayings holds in his hand
the crisis that judges him (τὸν κρίνοντα αὐτόν): the *logos*
that I spoke, this is what will judge (κρινεῖ) him on the last
day" (John 12:48). I therefore enter "already into crisis"
(ἤδη κέκριται, John 3:18) *before* my death because I encounter, standing before the word that Christ reveals, the three
conditions of a crucial crisis: the antagonism (to believe or
not; to lose one's life in order to gain it or the inverse), the
decision ("Today, if you hear his voice," or never), and
above all the judgment pronounced to me and about me—
for it is pronounced by me alone. In effect, I judge myself
and myself alone because "every one who does evil hates the
light, and does not come to the light, lest his deeds should
be exposed. But he who does what is true comes to the light,
that it may be clearly seen that his deeds have been wrought
in God" (John 3:20–21). What my death alone can never

bring to me—knowledge of the decision that concerns me—
the word of Christ, in his light, brings to me: I know the
decision concerning me since it is I and I alone who make
it. I know who I am according to whether or not I will expose myself to the light. He who offers the way, the truth
and the path also gives me the chance to decide absolutely—to work out the truth about myself through my decision about him.[20]

THE LAST JUDGMENT

The crisis completes itself, therefore, in a truly crucial crisis,
not because God would assume the function of judge—
according to the way in which men understand justice—but
because he exposes himself before us in such innocence and
such abandon that each of us must decide our own relation
to him—we each must decide *ourselves*. Standing before
Christ on the Cross, I cannot pass without taking notice, because even passing without taking notice constitutes a decision; I must therefore decide for myself: no one decides for
me, except me, and yet I decide for myself because I am confronted with the fact of Christ on the Cross. I decide for myself absolutely, though I emit no absolute judgment (I am
lacking the criterion, the power, and the right) about myself,
because I enter, standing before Christ, into a free crisis,
under the breath of the Spirit who "convicts the world concerning κρίσις . . . because the prince of this world has already been judged κέκριται)" (John 16:8–11). This self-
judgment can arise only before the silent face of Christ on
the Cross, and thus also before his annunciation by the believers (Romans 2:1–7); each announcement of the cruci-
fixion of Christ therefore provokes, in each moment of space
and place of time, the opportunity for each person to decide

---

[20] Ignace de la Potterie: "Judgment is therefore nothing other than the
rejection of the revelation brought by Jesus, the refusal to welcome his
word of truth. Such judgment is already condemnation, the *krisis* is a *ka-
takhrisis*" ("Jésus roi et juge," p. 241).

for himself: to reach, to know, and to settle his crisis. What we regularly name the Last Judgment holds no menace or horror, for it doubtless concerns the extreme limit of the delay generously allotted so that all souls may find their respective crises—to hear the Christ proclaimed, so as to perform, facing his word, the self-judgment. The Last Judgment states the promise that each will know who he is, because he will be who he will have truly decided to be. The long and arduous combat that we conduct with and among ourselves will have an end: we decide and will decide about ourselves on the occasion and as a result of Christ on the Cross: "Spiritual combat is as brutal as the battle of men; but the vision of justice is the pleasure of God alone" (Rimbaud).[21] And, to await this Judgment as well as to secure the one that each day imposes on us, it is remarkable that Christ gives himself as viaticum in order to keep us on the path of our self-judgment: for he who receives in Holy Communion the eucharistic species "eats and drinks judgment upon himself ($\varkappa\varrho\iota\mu\alpha$ $\dot{\epsilon}\alpha\upsilon\tau\tilde{\omega}$)" (1 Corinthians 11:29); the face always comes to us, without which we would in truth not be able to make our decision.[22]

We have been seeking a definition of crisis and its phenomenal figures. Beyond the apparent crises that politics and economics propose to us, beyond the incomplete crisis of my death, one single authentically accomplished crisis opens before us: that in which I must make my decision faced with Christ on the Cross—a crucial crisis in every sense. Christ alone opens for me the way to my own free crisis because he provokes it by the simple fact of exposing his life to the holiness of God—because he reveals himself simply as the Son that he is of God. God imposes and requires that I say either *yes* or *no* to his charity (Matthew 5:37); " Let your *yes* be *yes* and your *no*, *no*" (James 5:12), according to the model of he

---

[21] Arthur Rimbaud, "Adieu," *Une Saison en Enfer,* in *Oeuvres Complètes,* ed. A. Rolland de Renéville (Paris: Pléiade, 1963), p. 244.
[22] The judgment concerns only myself (faced with Christ) and therefore forbids me from judging the other (Matthew 7:2 = Luke 6:37). The two uses of judgment are joined in 1 Corinthians 4:3–5.

in whom all promises received their absolute *yes* (2 Corinthians 1:19). That to which Christ says such a *yes*, that in the face of which each is henceforward held to make his decision is named—charity. A single, complete, and performable crisis befalls us, in an identified conflict, decidable by a possible choice, and a choice that I can know: the crisis whose superabundance the Cross frees in the world, to the point of submerging it as the secret of its tragic character. Charity cannot, from the sole fact that it appears publicly, fail to cause a scandal and arouse a crisis. Whence a twofold paradox. First: only the crisis opened by the word of God said by Christ offers me free access to my own self-judgment and permits me to make my decision—in whatever sense this may be; which would no doubt mean that no man attains his crisis, and thus his final truth, if he does not confront Christ. Next: the crisis lets its scandal increase in proportion to the unconditioned but nonviolent power of the Cross: by the simple fact that it reveals itself, charity offers itself; by the fact that it offers itself, it instantly asks to be received; the more pressing, reiterated, and universal this demand becomes, the more it exposes itself to refusal—categorical refusal, refusal of the decision itself, it makes no difference, because the concern is with judging the possibility of self-judgment, and thus of condemning he who frees. For the death of Christ means not merely the murder of an innocent (which remains quite banal), and not merely the death of the perfect Innocent (M.-J. Le Guillou), but above all the death of he who exonerates the guilty. Charity alone is worthy of faith (H. U. von Balthasar), but, in calling for faith, it provokes the crisis—and the crucial crisis. To respond to our most intimate requirement—finally to know who I am—charity indissolubly provokes the crisis wherein I make my decision standing before it, and the crisis wherein I refuse it to the point of death; for I can prefer to die rather than to receive the charity to live. When the crisis of charity incites refusal, most often there arises, like a toxic, masking cloud between it and those who refuse it, speech about the "crisis." "The crisis," which is not one, offers the enormous advantage of happily leaving us impotent, undecided, calmly in agony: substituted for the crisis of charity are the "crises" of civilization, of morality, of the family, of the dollar, of natural resources, of oil, of the Middle East, and so on, in short of calm worries that concern me without making me decide to make my decision. The double-edged sword of violence that ravages the world frightens us less than the double-edged sword that Christ is said to have brought to earth: for the former brings the death we wish for, while we are afraid of the latter, which brings charity and judgment, and which we hate, so long as they remain foreign to us. Thus man divides himself against himself before God, when God grants him that which he thought he wanted and, in fact, fears—the crucial crisis: "Come then, and let us reason together, says Yahweh" (Isaiah 1:18). Brought to bear on our own historical situation, this paradox takes clear form. On the one hand, all of modernity can submit this diagnosis: "The particular crisis of man . . . consists in a growing lack of confidence in his own humanity."[23] All of modernity desires that man, having entered into a crisis through the superman within him, come to a crucial crisis. But our world is afraid of submitting to the sole crucial and completed crisis that there is, the word spoken by the Christ; thus the world evades the inevitable consequence that John Paul II emphasizes uncompromisingly: "The crises of the European are the crises of Christian culture."[24] Which means not so much that the crises of the one are identical to those of the other, as that, first and foremost, man will come to his true identity—and today he has hardly any time left to wait—only by exposing himself to the crucial crisis of charity.

3 July 1983

[23] John Paul II, *Discours à l'U.N.E.S.C.O.* (Paris, 2 June 1980), n. 13, *Documentation Catholique* 1788 (15 June 1980): 606. To lessen what might seem strange about this rapprochement, we allow ourselves to refer to our article "L'altro sguardo," in *La cultura, strumento di ripresa della vita* (Milan: Feltrinelli, 1982), the proceedings of a June 1981 colloquium dedicated to the cultural thought of John Paul II. The French text is found in *Pela Filosofia: Homenagem a Tarcisio Padilha* (Rio de Janeiro: Pallas, 1984), pp. 303 ff.

[24] "Discours au Vième Symposium des Evêques d'Europe," *Documentation Catholique* 1842 (19 December 1982): 1153.

6

The Gift of a Presence

EASTER INNOVATES, and does so radically. Either Christ no longer has any importance on this day, or "he brought all newness in bringing himself, who was announced in advance; for what was announced in advance was exactly this: that Newness would come to renew and revive man" (St. Irenaeus).[1] The innovation has a name—Christ—and a function—to render man new, as well as all the things of life. Since the Resurrection of Christ, we can say, and for once with neither naivete nor fear of refutation, that from now on nothing will be as it was before. Since the Resurrection of Christ, we thus must relearn everything, like children (or rather, also like an old person, overcome by newness). "Run, brother, the new world is before you!"—such has been, for two thousand years, the rallying cry of Christ (Philippians 3:13). We are thrown forward in a world too new for us. We have only too great a tendency to shelter ourselves by attempting to repeat the categories, reasonings, and habits of the former world. But we must have enough modesty and coherence to admit that, if the second Adam saves the world only by accomplishing a new creation—"If anyone is in Christ, he is a new creation: the archaic powers have passed and behold, new things are come" (2 Corinthians 5:17)—the "new creation" (Galatians 6:15) results directly from the Cross. The Cross thus puts our most elementary understanding of the world at the crossing of interpretations.

And what is more elementary than presence itself? Whether we are philosophers or not, we know presence at

---

[1] St. Irenaeus, *Adversus Haereses*, IV, 34, 1.

once, and we know only it: we approach all that is in the
world thanks only to the presence that we grant it by our
attention, and that it in turn honors by its permanence. What
is—thus, everything—is in that it is present. Secured, ex-
pected, or deficient, presence manifests itself by sight and
touch. We have the healthy habit of seeing and touching, of
touching or at least of seeing (even if only with the mind) all
the things which, only then, can enter into our world.
Christ, in his Paschal glory, "recapitulates all things in himself alone" (Ephesians 1:10) and should thus give us the
"presence (parousia) of the Son of Man" (Matthew 24:27).
Now, once the Resurrection has taken place, what presence
is given to us? We should not touch ("Do not touch me,"
John 20:17), even if, by Christ's condescension for their lack
of faith, certain men were able to touch him: "Put your fin-
ger here: behold my hands; put out your hand, and place it
in my side" (John 20:27). We see, finally, no more than an
absence: the void of the tomb (John 20:2), or the void of a
disappearance after the (sacramental) sign of recognition
(Luke 24:30–31): "He had become non-visible for them,
ἄφαντος, evanuit," or the, at last, final void of a "cloud"
(Acts 1:9) and a "heaven" (Luke 24:51), a sky where one
"sees no one" (Acts 9:7). Thus the access to the most elementary presence closes itself, at the very instant when,
nonetheless, the eschatological promises are fulfilled. No
doubt we admit, in faith, that "through the Resurrection,
the Revealer of the eschatological will of God became the
incarnation of the eschatological reality itself" (Wolfhart
Pannenberg).[2] But because of our very faith in the fulfillment
of all things (John 19:28 = 13:1), we are all the less able to
conceive the reason why "the incarnation of eschatological
reality itself" should be translated, paradoxically, by non-
presence—in short, by the contrary of the completed incar-

---

[2] Wolfhart Pannenberg, Grundzüge der Christologie (Gütersloh: Güter-
sloher Verlagshaus, 1966), p. 381; Jesus, God and Man, tr. Lewis L. Wilkins
and Duane A. Priebe (Philadelphia: Westminster Press, 1977), p. 367
(translation modified). See E. Schillebeeckx, Jesus: Die Geschichte von einem
Lebenden (Freiburg: Herder, 1977), p. 481.

nation. A temptation, crude but therefore all the more current and efficacious, would even incite us to "murmur" against God (Exodus 16:2): after the long absence that the messianic waiting involved, and after the fulfillment that in the end the Resurrection of the Crucified realizes, why impose on men the ordeal of a delay without foreseeable end (Acts 1:7 = Matthew 24:36)? Why annul the incarnated presence by a withdrawal that has for its effect only the tempting of our weak faith? Let us not underestimate this temptation, for its very crudeness has given rise to two answers that are just as current and unsatisfying.

The first comes from liberal exegesis, be it rationalist or fideist: the disappearance of the Resurrected would be the condition and the motive for the appearance of the Church; the mythical story of the Ascension fits within the overall tactics that enable the first community to overcome its disappointment with the indefinite deferral of the end of time. In short, eschatological impatience could be tempered only by a new myth—that of the Ascension.[3] The second comes from the philosophers: the Ascension would dissolve all the believers' empirical links with the Resurrected; after this forced ascesis, only the law would offer a way of access; and thus the spirit, in a finally purified interiority, could unfold. Therefore, the pure spiritual relation would open the way for a rational, moral, or even speculative relation between men and God. The flesh of Christ would have played only a pedagogic role, provisional, and henceforth consigned to the past.[4] These two answers meet their limit and their contrary

---

[3] Rudolf Bultmann, *Theologie des Neuen Testaments,* 2d ed. (Tübingen: Mohr, 1954), p. 46. For a summary of the exegetical and "theological" interpretations, see the preface to the classic work by Gerhard Lohfink, *Die Himmelfahrt Jesu: Intersuchungen zu dem Himmelfahrts— und Erhöhungstexten bei Lukas* (München: SANT, 1971), pp. 13–31.

[4] Immanuel Kant, *Religion innerhalb der Grenzen der blossen Vernunft,* III, 2; G. W. F. Hegel, *Vorlesungen über die Philosophie der Religion, Absolute Religion,* II, 3, in *Jubiläum Ausgabe,* ed. H. Glockner, XVI (Stuttgart: Fromanns Verlag, 1926), pp. 300–301; and *Phänomenologie des Geistes,* in *Gesammelte Werke,* IX, ed. W. Bonsiepen and R. Heede (Hamburg: F. Meiner, 1980), pp. 418–419.

in the consistent and continuous affirmation of the Christian law that it is "bodily" (*Symbol* of Epiphany, 325?), "with the flesh of his Resurrection and his soul" (*Symbol* of Leo, 1053), "each equally in the other" (*Lateran* IV, 1215), that Christ ascended into heaven.[5] In other terms, Christian faith rejects any "spiritualist" watering down of the Ascension, and thus demands also that the paradox be reinforced: putting aside the ordinary modes of presence (touch, sight) nevertheless does not exclude bodily presence. The Christian law claims to maintain bodily presence all the more radically, because from now on this flesh and this body belong fully and definitively to divinity. It is therefore not enough, if one wants to understand the mode of presence through absence that the Ascension inaugurates, to "spiritualize" presence by excluding the body, since the Ascension itself includes this body forever in God. Dualism (Platonic, gnostic, Cartesian, etc.) will be of no use to us. What is paradoxically offered for meditation consists not in a reduction of presence to the spirit, but in a reinforcement of the presence of the body and the spirit such that, in absence, both are incomprehensibly maintained, conserved, saved—in a word, resurrected. If the Ascension is worth pondering, in short if the Ascension offers a mystery, it does so by a radical modification of presence—by an effect of the Resurrection on presence in general. By a resurrection of presence.

LUKE: BLESSING

Backed against these requirements, let us read the sole uncontestable gospel text that relates to us the enigmatic event

---

[5] H. Denziger, *Enchiridion Symbolorum* (Freiburg: Herder, 1976), n. 13, 344, and 430, respectively. Whence Kant's deploring "the materiality of all the beings of the world," to which Karl Rahner retorts, quite justly, "We Christians are the most sublime materialists: we cannot, we should not, as a general rule, think any achievement of the spirit nor of actuality without at once thinking the permanence of matter and its fulfillment" ("Fest der Zukunft der Welt," in *Schriften zur Theologie*, VII [Zürich/Köln: Artemis Verlag, 1956], p. 181). This overturns the judgment that Marx

of the Ascension, Luke 24:50–53, in the intention of fore-seeing the dimensions or rather the axes that traverse this paradoxical presence—just as forces, applying their divergent tensions to a body, balance it or rather put it, in its apparent immobility, under tension. "Then he led them out as far as Bethany, and lifting up his hands he blessed them (εὐλόγη-σεν). And it happened that, in the very gesture of blessing (ἐν τῷ εὐλογεῖν), he took a distance from them (διέστη) and was carried up into heaven. As for them, after prostrating themselves before him, they returned to Jerusalem filled with great joy; and they were continually in the Temple, blessing God (εὐλογοῦντες)."

First remark: the point for Christ is to leave Jerusalem (and this world); and for the disciples to leave Jerusalem (where they were living hidden in fear), but finally so as to return there, this time openly and in the very midst of the Temple. Where does Christ go to leave Jerusalem and the world? Near Bethany. When, previously, according to Luke, had he come to Bethany? "And having spoken thus, he went up, walking first at their head (ἔμπροσθεν) to Jerusalem. When he drew near to Bethphage and Bethany" (Luke 19:28–29).[6] For Luke, as for all the evangelists, Bethany served as point of departure for the final entrance into Jerusalem, that is to say, inseparably for the popular triumph of Palm Sunday, the glorification in the Temple, and the Passion. Thus Christ left from Bethany, the first time, to glorify the Father in the Temple (and to receive a glorification) (John 12:27–36). This very glorification of the Father by Christ (and of Christ by the Father) provokes, at the end, the arrest and the putting to death, because the Jews cannot conceive it and especially cannot say it themselves like Christ did beneath their blind eyes. Moreover, Christ leaves them[7] as he charges them to

---

thought he could offer, among others, in opposition to Christians: "But love is a materialist, as non-critical as it is non-Christian" (Die Heilige Fam-ilie, IV, 3, in K. Marx and F. Engels, Werke, II [Berlin: Dietz Verlag, 1959], p. 22). In fact, love becomes truly materialist only in becoming Christian (ascension of a body).

[6] See also Mark 11:1, Matthew 21:1, and John 12:1.

[7] Matthew 24:1: "And, leaving the Temple, Jesus went away." See Luke 21:37 and Mark 13:1.

bless: "For I tell you, you will not see me again, until you say, 'Blessed is he who comes in the name of the Lord' " (Matthew 23:39, quoting Psalm 118:26).[8] Christ withdraws his presence (from the Temple, from Jerusalem) because the one sent by the Father, and thus the Father himself, does not receive the people's blessing. Presence depends directly on blessing: there where men do not bless the Father, the Father cannot make himself present; and for that matter, those who do not bless the Father not only do not bless He who comes in his name, nor the prophets, but they put him to death— after having put the prophets to death. There is no presence of God among men, if men do not bless him and the one he has sent. With Christ, this fundamental rule of revelation culminates in the eschatological crisis. Not that the blessing of men functions as the condition for the possibility of the presence of Christ—for Christ exposes his presence, even without blessing, to the final risk of being put to death. His blessing by men constitutes the condition for the possibility not of the presence of Christ, but of Christ's being recognized by them. Christ can give the present of his presence, without any condition; but so long as men do not bless God, this presence offered remains totally misunderstood, thus rejected and disfigured: "the world knew him not. He came among his own and his own received him not" (John 1:11); for "the world cannot receive him, because it does not contemplate him, οὐ θεωρεῖ, nor does it know him" (John 14:17). The presence of Christ, and therefore also that of the Father, discloses itself by a gift: it can therefore be recognized only by a blessing. A presence, which gives itself by grace and identifies itself with this gift, can therefore be seen only in being received, and be received only in being blessed.

Now we understand why the disciples must in turn go up to Jerusalem and why they must depart Bethany: Christ leads them back to the very point from which he departed in order to go up and have himself be recognized (in fact: mis-

---

[8] This same warning in Luke 13:34–35 concerns Jerusalem as such. Christ here takes up the words of Psalms 22:23 and 35:18.

recognized) by a crowd that could cry out quite well: "Blessed is he who comes in the name of the Lord!" (Psalm 118:26 = Luke 19:36 and parallels), but could not accomplish it in truth—really to bless to the point of acknowledging the gift of God. This very blessing that before Easter the people could not perform, after Easter and in virtue of the Resurrection, the disciples, first fruits of a new people, succeed, for the first time in the entire economy of salvation, in proclaiming: "They returned to Jerusalem with great joy; and they were continually in the Temple blessing God (εὐλογοῦντες τὸν θεόν)" (Luke 24:53).[9] Henceforward the disciples, that is to say the Church, that is to say humanity, finally reconciled with its destiny, no longer has but one function and one mission in a thousand different attitudes: to bless, so as thereby to welcome and acknowledge, the gift of the presence of God in and as his Christ.

Let us take care to understand the twofold and indissoluble meaning of the last words of Luke (and therefore of the first words of the Church, which speaks in Acts). In a first sense, because they bless the presence of he who "has gone up with a shout" (Psalm 47:5), the disciples, in replacing the crowd and constituting the new people, make possible the real entrance of Palm Sunday; because the people now bless the gift of the presence of Christ, Christ can really enter Jerusalem, the real Jerusalem, the heavenly Jerusalem. Without any paradox, it must be said that Christ rises up to the heavens *precisely because* the disciples, at last, bless at Jerusalem the gift of his presence.[10] But there is more: in a second sense, it must be said that the disciples could not truly bless he who comes

---

[9] See, e.g., Acts 2:47, 3:8, 4:21, and 21:20. Moreover, the story of the Ascension clearly adopts certain characteristics of the blessing of the Father by Christ in the Temple: address to the crowd (Acts 2:5), thunder in heaven (Acts 2:2, 2:6), and so on. Gerhard Lohfink evokes the paradigm of Ecclesiasticus 50:20 (see the entire development on εὐλογεῖν, pp. 167–169).

[10] This noteworthy judgment is by Heinrich Schlier, *Besinnung auf das Neue Testament,* XVI (Freiburg: Herder, 1964), p. 230. The act of blessing constitutes, by itself, the center of gravity and the framework that braces the entire text.

in the name of the Lord if they did not first themselves repeat Christ's gestures offering the paschal gift of his presence as God: to go up, from Bethany to Jerusalem, in order to bless God, before all the people and in the temple, for having made the bodily gift of his presence. By this repetition, they begin—for the first time—to accomplish in their own body that by which Christ received being the corporeal gift of the presence of God: the blessing of the Father. Having been spectators of the gift, they become for the first time the actors of the presence: received, incorporated into them (and above all them into it), given to all. If they receive the command no longer to "look into the heavens" (Acts 1:11), this is not only because it is now necessary to care for men. Or rather, they must do so only because they can; and they can only because they accede concretely—bodily—to the situation of Christ: in repeating his paschal ascent to Jerusalem, they too become "the fairest of the children of men" (Psalm 45:2), who "hid not [his] face from shame and spitting" (Isaiah 50:6). This identifying repetition will be accomplished, in flesh and blood, for the first time with the martyrdom of Stephen (Acts 6:8–15).

At this point, a new question arises, leading to a second remark. We can reconstruct the paschal ascent of the disciples to Jerusalem as the fundamental dimension of the presence given in the mystery of the Ascension, only by radically privileging the blessing of God by the disciples (Luke 24:53). Can these last words of the gospel nevertheless really constitute the final word of the presence given? Is the ultimate blessing of the disciples enough to account for the Ascension? Without a doubt it would not be enough if the disciples' blessing alone were at issue; but this blessing simply repeats, straightaway and strictly, a blessing that is alone foundational—that of the Resurrected. The Gospel of Luke marks this insistently, as the final word of his manifestations in this world: "and raising his hands, he blessed them. And it happened that, in the very gesture of blessing (ἐν τῷ εὐλογεῖν), he took a distance (διέστη) from them and was carried up into heaven" (Luke 24:51). Such an insistence, followed by the application of the same term to the disciples, clearly does not occur simply by chance. This raises two questions, the imbrication of which designates what is at stake in our reading. First question: What meaning does the blessing have when Jesus proclaims it, here and in general in the Gospel of Luke? Second question: What relation should we establish between the gesture of blessing and the taking of distance in the Ascension itself, for here the disappearance does not come after (as in Mark 16:19) the blessing, but at the same time—or better, *in* it? Trying to answer the first question amounts to seeking out when Jesus, according to Luke, pronounces a blessing. The most important occurrence of εὐλογ-εῖν appears in the story of the pilgrims at Emmaus: "taking the bread, he pronounced the blessing over it, broke it and gave it to them" (Luke 24:30). The same term already appeared during the multiplication of loaves (Luke 9:16 = Mark 6:41 and Matthew 14:19), in strict correspondence with εὐχαριστεῖν, to praise by offering thanks (Matthew 15:36 = Mark 8:6 and John 6:11 and 6:23). For the institution itself, Luke (22:17 and 22:19) abides by the common usage in the New Testament: εὐχαριστεῖω (Matthew 26:27 = Mark 14:23 = 1 Corinthians 11:24). These comparative similarities suffice to establish that the blessing, at the heart of which the Ascension is accomplished, cannot be separated from the Eucharistic blessing in general—the completed figure of the Father's blessing of men and of Jesus' blessing of the Father. Christ blesses fundamentally on the basis of his Eucharist to the Father, and in view of fulfilling it.

Now how, for Luke, after the Resurrection, is the eucharistic blessing of Christ carried out? Here the story of the pilgrims of Emmaus casts a surprising light on the ultimate blessing. In effect, the disciples, like the people in the Temple, rub shoulders with Christ without coming to recognize in him the gift of presence: the concrete corporeal proximity here prevents, rather than facilitates, the recognition that demands a blessing. When is it that "their eyes were opened" (Luke 24:31)? Not when they could see only an empirical and mute presence, but when a meaning, *the meaning*, led them to "recognize" (Luke 24:31) the gift of God. But such a meaning cannot directly manifest itself like an object subsisting and at the disposal of an indifferent and neutral spectacle; it manifests itself as a sign, which renders empirical reality symbolic of the invisibly incarnated reality—the eucharistic sign: "Once at table with them, taking the bread, he pronounced the blessing over it, broke it and gave it to them" (24:30). The Eucharistic sign provokes the corporeal presence of the spirit: in the institution narrative, this corporeal presence of the spirit (gift of presence) is accomplished first of all in the consecrated bread: "This is my body" (22:19); in the story of Emmaus, it is accomplished also and in addition in the recognition of Christ—namely: the recognition of the gift of the presence of God in *this* man, because this man can give himself to the point of abandoning himself like bread is distributed, abandoning himself like bread, like *this* bread, can concentrate all his presence in a gift, whether in a fleshly body or by taking body of the bread, always without any reserve whatsoever. In blessing, Christ makes himself recognized as gift of presence; the consecrated bread incarnates the perfectly abandoned gift of a "body given for [us]" (Luke 22:19). Thus Christ makes himself recognized—as gift of presence—ever since Easter by the sign of the blessing.

The eucharistic identification of the blessing in Luke permits us to draw a first conclusion: Christ, in blessing at the very moment of his ultimate elevation, and precisely because he disappears "in the very gesture of blessing," makes himself recognized as such by the disciples. Christ attests his divinity and makes it recognized in the very act of blessing. For him, to bless does not constitute one gesture, even religious, among other gestures, and that other men could accomplish just as well as he. The blessing makes recognized the holiness without equal and without measure of his relation to the Father. Thus he blesses when he recognizes with divine joy the mercifully paradoxical plan of the Father: "At that same hour he rejoiced in the Holy Spirit and said, 'I offer full thanks (ἐξομολογοῦμαι), to thee, Father, Lord of heaven and earth, that thou hast hidden these things from the wise and understanding and revealed them to babes. Yea, Father, for such was your gracious will. All has been delivered to me by my Father, and no one knows who the Son is except the Father, or who the Father is except the Son and any one to whom the Son chooses to reveal him' " (Luke 10:21–22). The absolute communion of the Son with the Father, as of the Father with the Son, alone can make them each appear as such; this recognition is accomplished in an inconceivable jubilation that the Spirit provokes (and attests): the blessing of the Father's will by Christ, from the most profound depths of his soul (as Word)—ἐξομολογοῦμαι. The ecstasy of this communion, in itself eternal, here becomes possible for the disciples: they see and hear, by human senses, an echo of the trinitarian joy: "Turning to the disciples he said to them privately: 'Happy are the eyes which see what you see' " (Luke 10:23; see Matthew 13:16).

The blessing, which here culminates in a confirmation and radical confession of the will of the Father, thus constitutes the unsurpassable instance of the recognition of Christ as Son by the Father through the Spirit, as well as of the recognition of Jesus as the Son by the disciples. The utterance itself of the ἐξομολογοῦμαι renders Christ recognizable. Here culminates what the baptism in the Jordan and the transfiguration already accomplished: the Father answers the Son's obedience with a recognition,[11] because, from the beginning to the end, the Son never stops blessing the Father with his obedience—thus his death confesses "with a loud voice" (Matthew 27:46 = Mark 15:37 and Luke 23:46) the gift of the Spirit yielded up to the Father (Matthew 27:50 = John 19:30). As a consequence, Christ leaves the disciples by blessing them and renders them for the first time capable of blessing only insofar as the very act of a full and total blessing makes him Son in the very eyes of the Father, and, in turn, makes him recognized in the eyes of the disciples. The disci-

---

[11] Matthew 3:17 and 17:5 = Mark 1:11 and 9:7 = Luke 3:22 and 9:35. Here the blessing comes from heaven instead of rising up to it; heaven, in each case, goes with the blessing. Likewise the cloud, which marks the flash of glory.

ples could not return to bless in Jerusalem, and for that matter would not have to, if such a blessing did not fulfill—in the depths of Christ's blessing—the entire filiation in spirit and truth that the Father ceaselessly awaits.

The eucharistic identification of the blessing in Luke opens a second possibility for interpreting the Ascension. During the eucharistic blessing at Emmaus, the resurrected Christ makes himself known by a sign—the consecration of the breaking of bread—that only his disciples can understand. But what exactly do they see in thus recognizing him? "Their eyes opened and they recognized him. And he himself became (ἐγένετο) invisible to them" (Luke 24:30–31). A strange paradox that is nevertheless found again, as is, in the Ascension: "And it happened (ἐγένετο) that, in the very gesture of blessing them, he took a distance from them" (Luke 24:51). If one admits our previous equivalence between the Eucharistic blessing and this ultimate blessing, the similarity of the two situations asserts itself: the blessing—which attests Christ as Son and as Resurrected—goes together with his sensible disappearance. Not only does it go together with the disappearance, but it also provokes it. And for that matter, with each blessing between the Father and the Son, is it not instantly recommended to the disciples to keep it quiet, to keep themselves quiet—if not to forget? Can we nevertheless go further in this mysterious chain of consequences? Let us note an evidence: the absolute accomplishment of the blessing signifies the absolute accomplishment, in the economy of the world, of the trinitarian communion; so long as this world remains subject to sin, a blessing between the Son and the Father passes beyond it, explodes it, in short annihilates it; therefore this blessing must be produced at a distance from our cosmic sin, for as long as the hour of Judgment does not arrive. And therefore Christ must remove from the gaze of the world (and even from his disciples) his communion of blessing with the Father for as long as the face of the world is not purified. Let us note a second evidence: the disappearance at Emmaus hides from the eyes of the disciples an unbearable glory, but nevertheless does not hide from them the presence of Christ; on the contrary, it gives it to them as the pure substantial gift of his body under the species of bread; and this presence remains not only real to them, but, if it dare be said, *more real* still than this physical presence of Christ. For Christ, even in the flesh, remains for them an individual, other, distinct, separated, who can "draw near" (Luke 24:15) to "walk with" them, who one may ask to "stay" (24:29), but with whom one is forbidden to unite oneself by the irreducible materiality of his body (for bodies do not unite, they separate). That this fleshly body disappears and leaves place for the eucharistic body of bread that one eats, that one assimilates to oneself, and which, in this unique case, assimilates to itself those who assimilate it (Augustine),[12] means: Christ becomes present, not to the senses (which cannot receive him, or even see him), but to the heart, burning from now on, and the mind, from hereafter understanding. The sensible disappearance allows the blessing to give the presence of Christ still more intimately, radically: the presence becomes still more of a gift, since it makes itself a gift communicable to the point of assimilation.

We can relate this paradoxical radicalization of the gift of presence to the Ascension: when Christ "took a distance" from the disciples, he clearly became *more*, and not less, present to them. Why? Because "with a great joy"—the very jubilation of Christ blessing the Father (ἠγαλλιάσατο, Luke 10:21)—the disciples hereafter accomplish the very blessing of Christ: they no longer watch Christ blessing, like indiscreet spectators (Luke 10:23); from now on, they themselves bless, as Christ blessed; they succeed in doing so only insofar as, hereafter, Christ blesses the Father in them. Like the body of Christ, his gesture becomes interior to them—constitutes them and creates them anew. Therefore, just as the invisibility at Emmaus did not hide the body of Christ (rather, it gave it perfectly), the withdrawal to a distance in the Ascension

---

[12] Saint Augustine: *"Cibus sum grandium; cresce et manducabis me, nec tu me in te mutabis sicut cibum carnis tuae, sed tu mutaberis in me"* (*Confessions,* VII, 10, 16). Other references can be found in Henri de Lubac, *Corpus Mysticum* (Paris: Aubier, 1949), pp. 200–202.

does not interrupt the economic action of Christ: Christ acts with and by virtue of the blessing of his disciples; he is forever working with them (Mark 16:20). Consequently, according to Acts, the "cloud" envelops him at the moment, not of giving the blessing, but of giving the mission—"You shall be my witnesses in Jerusalem and in all Judea and Samaria and to the ends of the earth" (Acts 1:8). In fact, giving the blessing amounts to giving the mission, for the mission consists only in the blessing; and the one like the other gives the perfect presence of Christ.

JOHN: DISTANCE

The presence of Christ therefore does not disappear with the Ascension, but is accomplished in it. It is accomplished as gift of presence, which abandons itself in the heart and the body of the disciples. Presence thus manifests itself as a gift precisely in that the man Jesus, empirically determined, "takes some distance." The Greek word used here by Luke, διίστημι, which Luke alone in the New Testament uses, deserves some attention. It suggests neither a total disappearance, nor an exaltation in the heights, but simply a retreat, a spacing, a step back.[13] That this taking of distance is nothing like a pure and simple absence is at once confirmed by the story of Acts: "This Jesus, who was taken up from you into heaven, will come in the same way as you saw him depart (πορευόμενον) for heaven" (Acts 1:11). The same way that allows for withdrawing and departing will become the way to come once again. Heaven is no longer anything like a screen or an inac-

[13] The word διίστημι suggests in Luke 22:59 an interval of time and in Acts 27:28 an interval of space. We are here following the analysis of the Lukean originality of the term given by G. Lohfink (p. 170). We maintain the authenticity of "He was carried up into heaven" (Luke 24:1) in following the opinion of H. Schlier. The Ascension marks less of a departure, a separation, or, indeed, an abandonment than the setting up of a gap (distance) crossed by the benedictions, first by the Spirit who doles them out. Without this gap and its distance, the blessings would not have been possible.

cessible place; it is forever opening itself, tearing itself open like the Temple curtain (Matthew 27:51), according to the prophet's desire: "O that thou wouldst rend the heavens and come down—before thy Face the mountains would quake" (Isaiah 63:19). If Christ goes up to heaven in order to return from there, from this moment on the vision of John is realized: "I saw heaven opened" (Revelation 19:11). This means that with the opening of heaven, God himself opens a two-way passage, God himself opens himself in the withdrawal of Jesus: "There is no more closed heaven. Christ is in heaven, which implies that God is accessible to man" (Joseph Ratzinger).[14] The Ascension does not signify the disappearance of Christ into the closed heavens, but the opening of heaven by a retreat that remains a mode of return. This paradox constitutes—ever since the beginning—the very mystery of the Ascension: "It is therefore at this moment . . . that the Son of man was known more excellently and more righteously as the Son of God; for having withdrawn in the glory of the paternal majesty, he began, in an ineffable way, to be more present through his divinity *(divinitate praesentior)*, he who had become more distant by his humanity. . . . When I will have gone up to my Father, you will touch me more perfectly and more truly *(verius)*."[15] The withdrawal of Christ does not make him less present, but more present than his physical presence permitted. Or rather, the new mode of his bodily presence (as the Eucharist) assures us, in the very withdrawal of the former body, a more insistent presence. How are we to understand that the insistent advance and the distant withdrawal thus coincide?

---

[14] Joseph Ratzinger, "Eschatologie—Tod und ewiges Leben," in *Kleine Katholische Dogmatik,* vol. 4, IX (Regensburg: Salvator Verlag, 1978), p. 118.

[15] Saint Leo the Great, *Sermo LXXIV* (61), 4 (in R. Dollé, ed., *Sources chrétiennes,* [Paris: Cerf, 1976], pp. 280–282). One can draw a comparison with the opinion of Joseph Ratzinger: "Based on the fact of the Ascension, Christ is not the one absent *(Abwesende)* from the world, but he who becomes present to it *(Anwesende)* in a new way" (*Lexicon für Theologie und Kirche,* V [Regensburg: Pustet, 1967], p. 361); or that of Karl Rahner (*Foundations of Christian Faith: an Introduction to the Idea of Christianity,* tr. William V. Dych [New York: Seabury Press, 1978], p. 181).

A text from the Gospels formulates just this paradox: "You have heard: I said to you, I go away (ὑπάγω) and I come to you (ἔρχομαι πρὸς ὑμᾶς). If you loved me, you would rejoice that I am taking the path to the Father (πορεύομαι πρὸς τὸν πατέρα), because the Father is greater than I" (John 14:28). One cannot lessen the strangeness of the project by introducing a chronological gap, for this text does not say, despite certain sanctioned translations: "I go away, and I will return," as if there were the temporal succession of a departure and then a return; it posits in strict contemporaneity the departure and the return, in the present: the Vulgate translates, "Vado, et venio ad vos." Nor can the edge be taken off this strangeness by supposing that the two verbs are synonyms, and create a redundancy. Indeed, "I am going away, ὑπάγω" always concerns the return to the Father. For instance: "I am with you yet a little longer and I go ὑπάγω to him who sent me" (John 7:33); "There where I go (ὑπάγω), you cannot go" (John 8:21); "There where I go (ὑπάγω) you cannot accompany me now" (John 13:36); "Now I go (ὑπάγω) to him who sent me" (John 16:5); "I go ὑπάγω to the Father, and you will see me no more" (John 16:10); "A little while, and you will see me no more, and again a little while and you will see me, for I go (ὑπάγω) to the Father" (John 16:17). The initial text, John 14:28, should therefore be explained in its full paradox: "I go away [to the Father who sent me and alongside of whom you do not have the capability to accompany me] and I come [at the same moment] to you." Christ comes toward us in the very moment, in the very measure in which he goes away to the Father. This is confirmed by the same text of the Gospel: "it is to your advantage that I go away" (John 16:7). The withdrawal is therefore useful to us, as the establishment of a distance.

But simply indicating the paradox is not sufficient to understand it. It is not so obvious, in human experience, that absence helps us to maintain, and still less to deepen, union with another. We know, by an experience as ordinary as it is awful, that removal almost always produces forgetfulness, desertion, and withdrawal. Our human loves die of absence and in the end we bear solitude better than separation. Separation always leads us into betrayal. Supposing that there are happy loves, they certainly are not separated loves. And yet, Christ claims exactly the opposite: "He who has my commandments and keeps them, he it is who loves me; and he who loves me will be loved by my Father, and I will love him and manifest myself to him (ἐμφανίσω)" (John 14:21); "If you keep my commandments, you will abide in my love, just as I have kept my Father's commandments and abide in his love" (John 15:10); "as thou, Father, thou art in me and I in thee, that they also may be one in us" (John 17:21).

The withdrawal of Christ has a precise intention: it is not a question of leaving behind him a pure absence, or a heart-rending memory, but of inscribing the gift of his commandments within "The virginal, vibrant, and beautiful today" (Mallarmé). Commandments, or rather instructions, like those that a director gives to his actors so that, without him (while he remains behind the scenes or even absent from the theater), they can mount the play, give life to the author's text, become themselves the characters that they dreamed of being. The directives must be executed, or performed: the text and the roles must be played, or performed. The play must be staged—that is to say, performed, as every English speaker knows when using the word *performance* for a theatrical event. Why perform the instructions? Not in order piously to execute a testament or the last wishes of one condemned to death, but—because it is a matter of one condemned to be resurrected—in order to live the same life that led him to die and to be resurrected. In effect, the instructions left by Christ do not give subaltern orders that he himself never executed; they record the gestures, the dispositions and the intentions that he himself in his humanity as well as in his divinity was constantly accomplishing to perfection. In accomplishing them with respect to men, he performed, within time, perfect love with respect to God, just as in eternity—with respect to the Father: "so that the world may know that thou hast sent me and hast loved them even as thou hast loved me" (John 17:23). When, therefore, the ultimate direction is given to the disciples—"I give you a new commandment: love one another. Yes, as I have loved you, you too, love one another" (John 13:34); "This is my commandment: love one another as I have loved you" (John 15:12)—the point is not simply, nor first of all, a moral injunction (even sublime and already Kantian); it is a matter of having done, by men, what Christ did with respect to them, in order to testify to what he does eternally with respect to his Father: "O righteous Father, the world has not known thee, but I have known thee" (John 17:25). Christ has known, that is to say blessed (εὐλογεῖν), through a Eucharist drawn from the depths of his soul (of the Word— ἐξομολογεῖν) the will of the Father; he manifested this absolute union by the unconditional and completed fulfillment of his love (John 17:1 = 19:28) to the end, as much for God as for men. If therefore the disciples keep this unsurpassable commandment, if they perform in truth and reality this ultimate direction, they themselves will play the role of Christ: "By this all will recognize you as my disciples, by this love that you will have for one another" (John 13:35).

Christ's departure allows for performing of the instructions in full responsibility, but the instruction to love has the disciples do the very thing that Christ accomplished; the disciples become the actors of charity, no longer passive and obtuse spectators of Jesus. With the gestures of the absent choragus, with their voices uttering the words of the absent author (the Word), with their faces modeled on the face of the invisible glory (invisible to the world), they come to the very performance of charity. And as charity alone is expressed in a single sense (the sole univocal), they accede to the role (persona), and thus to the personality of Christ. And Christ from now on holds them as his equals—by grace: "No longer do I call you servants, for the servant does not know what his master is doing; I call you friends, for all that I have learned from the Father, I have made known to you" (John 15:15). From this moment on, Christ's taking of distance—in death, in the Resurrection standing before Mary Magdalene and at Emmaus, and finally in the Ascension—

delivers its meaning: it is all about freeing the trinitarian role of the Word in order to make it accessible to the disciples, about arranging for them a "loosening of the reins" so that, alone, they accomplish the role of (adoptive) sons of the Father; it is about installing them at the very center of the filial role in a radically trinitarian play. Only the withdrawal of Christ out of this world permits the disciples' entrance into the space of the Trinity.

However, this "pedagogic" interpretation, in its initial correctness, remains too narrow. Besides the fact that it could open the way for the philosophical deviation stigmatized earlier, it does not take into consideration the moment of radical positivity in the Ascension. Christ in effect grants the disciples the privilege of playing his trinitarian role, and of thus becoming Christs, "Christians" (Acts 11:26 = 1 Peter 4:16), not only by the negative act of his taking distance in relation to us, but above all by the eminently positive act of crossing this distance. The distance between the trinitarian and Christic place, left (promised!) to the disciples and the exalted Crucified one, would have no meaning and no reality if several conditions were not met.

It is first necessary that the disciples have in their hearts the strength to play their role, as well as in mind the "spirit" of what they will perform—that is, they need the Spirit. It is also necessary that the trinitarian place opened to the disciples by the temporal withdrawal of Christ be simply tenable, habitable, practicable, in short that Christ has in fact triumphed over death, that in fact the love of the Father has through him annihilated the sin of the world—in other words, the Resurrection is necessary. It is necessary that Christ himself never stop acting, living, and loving, so that the distance he puts between himself and the disciples always maintains them in him, but also that he himself, now with his human body and soul, radiate with divine glory—which is to say, the Trinity is necessary. When Christ leaves this world, therefore, his withdrawal can free a trinitarian role for the disciples only in the strict degree to which it is coupled with an ascent toward the Father, where, through the ascen-

sion first of Calvary, then through the return from Hell and
the exaltation out of the tomb, and finally through the disappearance into heaven, he accomplishes, once and for all and
from the depths of human flesh, the trinitarian play. It is necessary that Christ himself make real what his promise to the
disciples made possible for them; he must perform the trinitarian gesture from the depths of humanity, from sin and thus
from death. In short, the Father can, at the request and in
the name of Christ, give the Spirit to the disciples only provided that it is indeed the same trinitarian Spirit that Christ
offers to the Father in breathing his last breath: "And *I* will
pray the Father, and *he* will give to you another Paraclete, to
be with you forever, the Spirit of truth, whom the world
cannot receive" (John 14:16–17); "the Paraclete, the Holy
Spirit, whom the Father will send *in my name*, will teach you
all things and will remind you of all that I have said to you"
(John 14:26); "When the Paraclete comes, whom *I* shall
send to you from the Father, the Spirit of truth, who proceeds from the Father, he will bear witness to me" (John
15:26); "It is to your advantage that I go away; for if I do
not go away, the Paraclete will not come to you; but if I go,
I will send him to you" (John 16:7).

If Christ leaves, it is in order to free the trinitarian site for
the disciples. But this site will become truly trinitarian only
if Christ accomplishes, at the core of his humanity, and thus
in the name of ours, the absolute trinitarian return of the Son
to the Father—and therefore only if he dies and returns to
life. Only on the basis of this economic performance of the
Trinity can the Spirit pour himself out economically and
without reserve on the disciples in the name of the Son, by
the Father—precisely because, even in the economy, the Son
and the Father have intermingled their wills in the one and
only Spirit. The outpouring of the Spirit into the world only
becomes possible because, by his departure toward the
Father and across death, Christ has introduced the trinitarian
play into the world, or rather has reintroduced the world
into its trinitarian and filial site (fixed by creation, but repu-
diated by sin). Christ does not withdraw simply for the bene-

fit of the disciples, he will reconquer the Spirit for them—a wholly other fire, for a wholly other Prometheus. Thus the very gesture that renders truly trinitarian the site opened to the disciples also renders it actually practicable for them. For the disciples could neither accomplish the proper gestures nor utter the appropriate words if the Spirit, invisible by definition but present by grace, did not guide them.

In order better to conceive it, let us return to the analogy of the theater: the disciples must play the role of Christ by loving each other mutually to the point of making Christ recognizable in them; however, this direction imposes on them no text written *ne varietur* and to be recited, no fixed script, no stereotypical *mise en scène*; one must improvise freely on the given theme: the Christian life unfolds as a *commedia dell'arte*, according to a free innovation that never ceases to perform the only love story in the history of the universe. The disciples could not be correct in their playing of the most supremely free, because trinitarian, role that Christ concedes to them if the Spirit did not inspire in them the gestures and the words. The Spirit confirms them, just as the prompter at the theater helps the actors and puts them at ease: "When they deliver you up, do not be anxious how you are to speak or what you are to say: what you are to say will be given to you straightaway, for it is not you who will speak, but the Spirit of your Father who will speak in you."[16] The Spirit inspires the disciples with the grace and the genius of their trinitarian role: it gives them enough courage to speak, like Peter, to the crowd of nations; enough surety to

---

[16] Matthew 10:19–20. See Mark 13:11, Luke 12:11, and John 14:26. In Luke 21:15, Christ (and not the Spirit) promises himself to inspire the disciples with answers: "I myself will give to you a language and a wisdom, which none of your adversaries will be able to withstand or contradict." The comparison that we are drawing between the prompter at the theater and the Spirit who inspires has, of course, a limit: the prompter brings to a failing memory a text *already* written, while the Spirit suggests to a freedom (that it itself frees) the force of a perfectly innovative gesture and the understanding of an unheard-of word. For the text can always be improved because it has a finite author, whereas the Spirit can, ad infinitum, modify and rejuvenate the face of the world, in short blow where it wills and what it wills—that is, what the trinitarian concert wills.

heal, to consecrate the bread, to pray; enough rectitude to
know how to answer the Jews and to die while blessing, like
Stephen. Christ, on the day of the Ascension, "took a distance from them." This distance, here manifested cosmolog-
ically by a disappearance into the "clouds," in fact constitutes
an essential and, since the Last Supper, constant dimension
of the mission of Christ. Distance allows the disciples to become not servants but friends, not spectators but actors of the
redemptive and revelatory action of Christ. They themselves
occupy the place, the role, and the charge of Christ. They
could not do so, however, if the distance were limited to a
withdrawal; in fact, it completes the trinitarian accomplishment that delivers Christ to the Resurrection, the humanity
of Jesus to glory, and the Spirit of the Father to the disciples
of the Son. Thus, as much by the Eucharist as by the gift of
the Spirit, the withdrawal of the Ascension makes the disciples come unto a perfect, though paradoxical presence in
Christ.[17] Paradoxical, for this presence no longer admits any
sensible support and, for outside observers, reduces to pure
and simple absence. Perfect, precisely because this presence
no longer consists in seeing another, even the Christ, loving,
dying, and returning to life, but oneself, like him, in him,
according to him, actually loving, dying, and returning to
life. Presence: not to find oneself in the presence of Christ,
but to become present to him (to declare oneself present,
available) in order to receive from him the present (the gift)
of the Spirit who makes us, here and now (in the present),
bless him like he blesses the Father—until and in order that
he return. The highest presence of Christ lies in the Spirit's
action of making us, with him and in him, bless the Father.

MATTHEW: MISSION

The high and paradoxical presence of Christ that the Ascension establishes is understood only by means of a step back

---

[17] See Hans Urs von Balthasar, *Herrlichkeit, Theologie 2* (Einsiedeln: Jo-
hannes Verlag, 1969), p. 363.

from economy into the Trinity. Or more exactly, it attests the inscription of our world in a Christic site, and thus, after the Resurrection, in a manifestly trinitarian site. The presence stemming from the Resurrection definitively overcomes the categories of ordinary presence in the world. Thus Christ is neither present in visible flesh, nor absent yet present in spirit or memory only, since his Eucharistic body is given to us daily.

He gives himself, as a present, according to the Spirit. This Spirit does not offer an abstract and malleable spiritualization of this present; on the contrary, it is forever working to erect a body for it—and a multifaceted body: that of the Eucharist, that of the Church concretely built of men, even that of the humanity of Jesus eternally glorified. In a word, as the gift of the presence of Christ comes from the hither side (or the beyond) of this world, he can, subsequently, set himself forth according to a power without analogue, one that passes beyond the limits of worldly presence. Here it is necessary to give full weight to an apparently trivial remark: if Christ had remained physically among us, according to the worldly economy of presence, he would have fixed himself in a place and a time; he therefore would have been inaccessible to men of all ages and all places. This empirical impossibility of encountering him would then have merely reflected a still more radical impossibility of recognizing him: had we approached him, we would not have been able—without the sending of the Spirit, because without trinitarian fulfillment—to recognize him; for we do not bless him, and in him the Father, except through the Spirit. We therefore owe our seeing him to the gift, through the Spirit and in the trinitarian distance of the presence of Christ—in Spirit and in Truth, in all places and in all ages.[18] We see (recognize, bless)

---

[18] That the worldly conditions of presence become outmoded is indicated, in a contrasting play, by the material transgressions (John 20:19 and 20:26), the contrary proofs of materiality (Luke 24:37–43 = John 20:20, 20:27, 21:10–12). The Spirit reproduces this play (Acts 2:1–2), but so do the disciples (Acts 5:19, 12:6–11, 16:25–40). Neither in conformity with nor contrary to the worldly modes of presence, the gift of presence plays otherwise.

Christ only because he "took a distance" from us. Whence the strict connection of the Ascension with the sending of the disciples on mission. The mission does not compensate for the immediate physical absence of Christ by a conquering, fanatic, and anxious imperialism; the whole resurrection of the presence as a gift has for its goal to render the mission possible—universal gift of the presence of Christ, which presupposed first that the presence would become a gift. Even more, it must be said that the sending on mission constitutes the preeminent performance of the gift of presence: the disciples play their Christic role by giving the presence of Christ universally. This close connection between the Ascension and the mission is clearly marked in Acts: "Receive the power of the Holy Spirit that comes over you, and be for me witnesses in Jerusalem, in all Judea and Samaria and to the end of the earth" (Acts 1:8), as well as in the long final passage of Mark: "And he said to them, 'Go into all the world (ἅπαντα), proclaim the Good News to all creation (πάσῃ τῇ κτίσει)'. . . . So then the Lord Jesus, after having spoken to them, was taken up into heaven and seated at the right hand of God. As for them, they went forth and preached in all places (πανταχοῦ), the Lord acting with them and confirming the Word by the miracles that accompanied it" (Mark 16:15–20).[19] As for John, it announces the Ascension: "Do not touch me, go to my brethren and say to them that I am going up (ἀναβαίνω, ascendo) to my Father and your Father, to my God and your God" (John 20:17). We must emphasize that in these two speeches the disciples find themselves exactly situated in the trinitarian site of Christ, wherein they become brothers through one and the same Father.

However, we owe to the conclusion of Matthew, which precisely does not mention the episode of the Ascension, the clearest connection of the gift of presence and the sending

---

[19] The verb used here (v. 15: πορευθέντες) is the same as that which, in John 14 and 16, expresses the paradoxical outward-bound coming of Christ toward his disciples. For the disciples henceforth go to the nations announcing this same going and coming Christ, through the Eucharistic presence and the Spirit.

on mission. To grasp this, we must draw out cleanly the chronological, but also the theoretical, moments of this text.

1. *Encounter.* At the initiative of Christ, who wants not to have himself be seen but recognized, the disciples "see" only in order to "prostrate themselves" (Matthew 28:17 = Luke 24:52), at least if they believe. This is not in any way about a spectacle, but about what Luke indicates by the blessing. The presence of Christ hereafter comes from the hither side of the world, from its trinitarian fulfillment.

2. *Power.* Christ comes to say to the disciples nothing other than the plenitude of his presence, completely accomplished in the trinitarian distance, and which, from now on starting from "the bosom of the Father" (John 1:18), can erupt into this world too narrow for it only as an omnipotence given by the Father: "All the power (πᾶσα ἐξουσία) in heaven and on earth has been given to me" (Matthew 28:18). Power given—by the Father, in virtue of the Paschal crossing of distance, in the sense where it is "a loud voice in heaven" that proclaims "the Kingdom of our God and the ἐξουσία of his Christ" (Revelation 12:10) and in which it is, after his similarly paschal kenosis, "God who has highly exalted him and bestowed on him the name which is above every name, that at the name of Jesus every knee should bend, in heaven and on earth and in Hell" (Philippians 2:9–10). Prime totality, and the most radical: the total power of a presence totally converted into gift, given to the Father, given over to the Son, givable through the Spirit to the disciples.[20] The power of the divine presence, given and received trinitarily, will give itself superabundantly according to a threefold totality, which saturates the world.

3. *Totality of the teaching*: "Teaching them to observe all (πάντα) that I have commanded you" (Matthew 28:20).

---

[20] In this sense, the *pantocrator* (2 Corinthians 6:18; Revelation 1:8, 4:8, etc.) should be understood only as a presence given by the Father from the other side of the world, and received totally as a gift (not as a ἁρπάγμος or a *rapina*) by Christ, in such a way that he can in his turn communicate it as totally as he wants (and thus infinitely), and men can receive it (and thus very little, at least in this time).

The instructions to observe in order to act the play of Christ correctly reduce to the "new commandment" that accomplishes everything—but that only all things, which no book could ever contain (John 20:30 = 21:25), would suffice to illustrate. The totality thus claimed by the prescribed teaching signifies that the truth is revealed in advance, superabundantly, and that, standing before its given presence, every previous theological interpretation will no doubt be possible, and thus requisite, but obsolete.

4. *Totality of space*: "Go (πορευθέντες) and teach all the nations (πάντα τὰ ἔθνη), baptizing them in the name of the Father, of the Son, and of the Holy Spirit" (Matthew 28:19). The eschatological promise of the prophets can only be reconciled with the doctrine of the "remnant of Israel" if the latter is concentrated in God's one and only Christ, who himself is not counted among the nations and the groups, since he comes from God, and, through the Ascension, returns to him. Universality can legitimately characterize the disciples' mission only to the degree to which he who is announced does not belong to the world. Baptism can claim to be universal—by right—only insofar as it is given on the basis and in view of the Trinity. The mention here of the "Father, of the Son, and of the Holy Spirit" could be surprising, to the point that certain exegetes have doubted its authenticity. From the point of view of theological rigor, however, no hesitation is permitted: unless it were to sink into the ambient raving imperialism, unless it were to fall back into the most nationalistic political messianism, it was fitting that the universality of the baptismal mission arose from beyond the world, thus from the Trinity: the inscription of Christ, as Son, in a trinitarian site manifests itself in the world only with the Paschal exaltation, and thus at the time of the Ascension. As soon as this origin and this site are misunderstood, it becomes inevitable that the mission of a universal baptism will be put into question—in the name of the relativity of times, of civilizations, and of cultures. But, in contrast, the Ascension (understood in a trinitarian fashion) radically demythologizes all cultural relativism, as well as all

imperialistic deviations (inverted errors, born from a common misunderstanding).

5. *Totality of times*: "Behold, I am with you all (πάσας) the remaining days, to the consummation of time" (Matthew 28:20). How could Christ come to us, in each moment, in presence, if it were a matter of his historically bounded presence, about which he tells the limit, in the same gospel: "You will always have the poor with you, but you will not always have me with you" (Matthew 26:11; see Mark 14:7 and John 12:8)? He can come to us only because, from the trinitarian site, the Spirit in each moment grants the disciples to act like Christ, in the name and the role of Christ; his assistance joins with the inscription of the disciples in the Christic function, and with, on their part, the use of time for prayer "in every moment (πάντοτε)" (Ephesians 5:20).[21] This elevation of the disciples has reality only with the exaltation of Christ, who thus consecrates the economic insertion of the Trinity. Henceforth Christ comes to the disciples in each moment, because he comes to them from beyond time—from whence likewise he can come at the end of this same time. Alpha and Omega, because preceding time from the very heart of the Trinity.

The totality of ἐξουσία therefore sets itself forth in terms of a threefold totality: the totality of the teaching, the totality of space, the totality of time. Their totalization consists in "gathering all things (τὰ πάντα) under a single head, in Christ, all things in the heavens and on earth" (Ephesians 1:10). This recapitulation is distinguished from all totalitarian drift, for at least two reasons. First because, for Christ, it is a matter of reinvesting his own property—creation—which thus does not suffer the violence of a mercenary, but instead rediscovers the benevolent guardianship of a shepherd who actually dies for it. This very royalty only has meaning in offering the world to the Father, and thus completing the proper return of the Son to the bosom of the Father; the to-

---

[21] "Always" defines the temporality of the disciples in Romans 1:10, I Corinthians 1:4, Philippians 1:4, and Colossians 1:3.

tality passes to the Son only in order to pass to the Father, as
and with him, in an analogous manner of exaltation: "And
when all things (τὰ πάντα) are subjected to him, then the
Son himself will submit to Him who submitted all (πάντα)
to him, so that God might be all in all (πάντα ἐν πᾶσιν)" (1
Corinthians 15:28). With the result that the recapitulation
does not merely render to God all that is outside God—
creation—but at last offers to him, like praise, a work that
reflected his glory: the recapitulation (with the world), like
the Ascension (with Jesus), offers God to God. Next, the recapitulation, which the Ascension opens and the mission
carries out, is fulfilled under the rule of distance or, what
here amounts to the same thing, of the gift of presence.
Therefore each baptism, each conversion, each consecration
manifests only indirectly the presence of Christ: the disciple
announces the master, though obscurely; and in this mimetic
announcement, he sketches out a presence that withdraws,
and diverts until the end of time the consummation of his
glory: "Our citizenship is in heaven, and from it we ardently
await, as savior, the Lord Jesus Christ who will transfigure
our miserable body" (Philippians 3:20); "Your life is hidden
with Christ in God; when Christ, your life, will be manifest,
then you also will be manifest with him in full glory" (Colossians 3:3–4); "Beloved, we are God's children now, but
what we shall be has not yet appeared. We know that when
he will be manifest, we shall be like him" (1 John 3:2). Presence will be totally recapitulated only when the gift of the
Father will be totally granted us. The Ascension puts into
operation the recapitulation of the totality, but only the
Father knows the day and the time of the completed manifestation, because this ultimate presence can only be
given—by him.

Thus the Ascension does not mark the disappearance of
Christ in the expectation of a new (empirical) presence at the
end of an all too long absence. It marks the Paschal conversion of all presence into gift: blessing, submission to the
Spirit which makes us act in and as Christ, and mission in
totality constitute the three dimensions of the gift of pres-

ence in distance. For if the Word became flesh, it is necessary, ever since the Ascension, that, in us, "flesh become word—and the word fall" (Octavio Paz).[22] Our flesh becomes word in order to bless the trinitarian gift of the presence of the Word, and to accomplish our incorporation in Him.

February 1983

---

[22] Octavio Paz, "Pasado en claro" (1975); translated in *A Draft of Shadows and Other Poems* (New York: New Directions, 1979), p. 143.

7

What Love Knows

I

THOUGH EXPLICITLY DECLARED "the greatest" (1 Corinthians 13:13) of theological virtues, though raised to the rank of the last of the divine names—for "God is charity" (1 John 4:16)—charity remains profoundly misunderstood by modern Christianity. We have recognized ourselves in faith: faith suits us, because it affirms at the risk of affirming itself, bestows upon us an identity among men and a project on the world, allows for the celebration and proclamation of the name of God from the rooftops, even moves mountains and cities. In short, faith, with its properly theological dignity (and more), seduces by the strength and the confidence it grants to human incertitude. In nostalgic appeals to a once-dominant and self-assured Christianity—doubtless more a fantasy than a reality—as well as more recent dreams of "re making Christians of our brothers," we have always put our confidence in faith. We recognize ourselves even more today in hope: a little flame, of course (so very true to Péguy's image), stripped bare of sumptuousness, of power, and even of doctrine, marginalized and lost amid a crowd that knows nothing of it, yet quick to interpret the least movement as a "sign of the times," the obstinate nightlight of an ever benevolent hermeneutic, never despairing despite being disappointed most of the time. In a word, hope, which presupposes nothing gained because it has only to wait, attracts because of the humble serenity it dispenses to our common anxiety. In our desire for a future Christianity that would at last be majoritarian and reconciled with modernity—an ambiguous dream, for though Christ promised the Church that the gates of Hell would not prevail against her, he never guaranteed her universal triumph, if only because he himself tolerated the triumph of Palm Sunday simply in order to demonstrate its perverse illusion—it is in hope that we place our expectations.

Faith is organized according to the past requisites of Revelation, through tradition. Hope unfolds in accord with Revelation's obligatory future, through mission. There remains the present—the *here and now* of Revelation, the instant ceaselessly proposed anew, in which we are able to see whether and to what extent we are becoming disciples of Christ. A present that has nothing of the nicely wrapped present about it, because it clears the space of truth in which, each time, for us alone if not for the public, we experience without any doubt whether or not "we are rooted and grounded in Christ's charity" (Ephesians 3:17). Indeed, charity plays itself out in the present: in order to know if I love, I need not wait, I have only to love; and I know perfectly well when I love, when I do not love, and when I hate. Contrary to the certitude of faith, which requires time for perseverance (St. Augustine) and the final revelation of what we already are (Colossians 3:3–4), and unlike the certitude of hope, which will only find its reward in the last days (Matthew 24:42–51), charity waits for nothing, commences right away, and is fulfilled without delay. Charity manages the present. And the present, seen from the point of view of charity, signifies also, and before all else, the gift. Charity renders the gift present, presents the present as a gift. It makes a gift to the present and a gift of the present in the present.

This, no doubt, is the reason why charity disheartens us, worries us, and taxes us: because, when it comes to charity, no excuse, no way out, no explanation is of any avail. I love or I do not love, I give or I do not give. It is certainly no accident that all the parables of the Last Judgment hinge not on faith—the righteous being the faithful believers, the unjust the miscreants—nor on hope—the righteous hoping for the restoration *in fine* of the Kingdom of Israel, the others having given up on it—but on charity. Have we helped our neighbor, given even from our surplus, loved the least among us? This is the only criteria, the only crisis, the only test. The Judgment singles out not the athletes of faith, nor the militants of hope, but the workers of charity. By consequence, charity becomes for each of us the site of an individual Judgment that, in the end, includes the whole span of time that we call our life. Following the Johannine theology of the Judgment, our judgment remains immanent: we judge ourselves by freely taking a definite position before the word of Christ, without any extrinsic condemnation, so that at each moment we choose, patiently and decisively, whether we love Christ or hate him—"I did not come to judge the world . . . [but] he who scorns me and does not receive my sayings has a judge: the word that I have spoken, and it will judge him on the last day" (John 12:47–48). A disturbing doctrine, which puts everything in our hands; all the more disturbing in that it concerns the simplest act—to love or not to love. For our nearest neighbor—*"Interior intimo meo"*—is always Christ. Thus we judge ourselves according to whether we are charitable to charity—that is, the charity to love him. We are afraid of charity because, above all, it gives us notice to love, or not, the One who enables us to love: the Christ. So it happens that sometimes we do not love charity. Whence this fundamental law of the world: "love is not loved."

II

Charity, love—we have just imperceptibly passed the boundary that, in principle, separates them. Everyone knows it is necessary to distinguish carefully charity, the theological virtue, from love, the passion of man *in via*. But the philosophical tradition has imposed its own divisions. The most established distinguishes between love as a passion of the soul, and intellectual love.

In its first determination, love signifies a passion among

others, which is to say (following Descartes)[1] a perception provoked by the body (hence irrational) that affects the soul (and thus merits the title of perception), in such a way that the soul attributes it to itself (and not to its body or to other bodies). Like all the other passions, love thus becomes a confused perception, absolutely governed by the subjectivity that it affects, starting with its body; as Spinoza will make explicit, this general character of closed subjectivity (from my body, in my soul, toward my soul) results from passion's incapacity to know an external end: the inadequate and confused knowledge that Peter has of Paul allows him to know better the state of mind (the subjectivity) of Peter, than to know anything whatsoever of Paul.[2] Thus, in general, passion masks the other and only makes use of him in order to mark the subjectivity that it affects. If love constituted a passion only in this sense, it would regress to the rank of a solipsism, which closes rather than opens access to anyone else. But there is more. Among all the passions, it falls to love to accomplish this solipsism in the most radical manner. Let us take the definition of love proposed by Descartes: the passion which consists in considering oneself as forming a part of a whole, of which the beloved furnishes the other part; all loves are hierarchically arranged solely according to the variations in the relative importance of one part (me) or the other (the beloved), the structure itself unvarying; thereafter, between the loves in which I constitute the greater part of the whole (love of the bottle, of a woman taken by force, or of hoarded money) and those in which I constitute only the lesser part (love of one's wife, children, prince, or God), the differences in the objects only underscore the invariant structure. As a consequence, all these forms of love "are sim-

---

[1] René Descartes, *Passions de l'âme*, §27–29, in *Oeuvres philosophiques*, ed. Adam-Tannery [Paris: Vrin, 1906 [1966]) XI, pp. 349–350; *The Philosophical Writings of Descartes*, vol. 1, tr. John Cottingham, Robert Stoothoff, and Dugald Murdoch (Cambridge: Cambridge University Press, 1985), pp. 338–339.

[2] Baruch Spinoza, *Ethica*, II, §17; *The Ethics and Selected Letters*, tr. Samuel Shirley (Indianapolis: Hackett, 1982), p. 78.

ilar,"[3] because they all reduce to the same act of the will, by which the *ego* unifies itself with an object, whatever it may be. Seen through such a lens, love sets in motion only a confused representation and an arbitrary will. Not only does subjectivity not necessarily love a true good and, most often, an illusion of the good, it above all loves nothing that differs from it: first of all because, in a passion, it generally has no clear and distinct knowledge, and next because the act of will can apply to any object, loveable or not, loving or not, human or not, and so forth. In such a love, in fact, what is missing, along with knowledge, is the other himself. In the best of all cases, the other (wife, child, prince, or God) merely provides the occasion for a union of will that is irrational (by virtue of passion) and solipsistic (by virtue of the primacy of subjectivity). Love is defined by its ignorance of the other.

We should not be surprised by such a paradox—it has been widely illustrated and exploited by modern literature. Sticking with the best-known examples, from Stendhal to Proust, the amorous hero suffers a passion that, confirming Spinoza, describes much more obviously the state of his own subjectivity than this other whom he nevertheless claims to love so much that he would sacrifice and throw over everything for her. Passion is born of the desire, the imagination, the timidity, the admiration, the audacity—of he who loves; it grows all the more as its object stays far away, unavailable, missing—in short, does not appear, and indeed, is not. Reciprocally, passion ceases as soon as its object becomes, for the first time, visible as such: when *she* at last shows or offers herself, the principal of reality that she puts into motion defuses a passion that, precisely, fed itself solely on her unreality (Flaubert). This literary plot in fact announced the fate reserved for love in present day public life. Contemporary amorous discourse is marked by an evidence and a silence that are equally massive. First of all, the evidence: the proliferation of objects deemed able to awaken love, or at least to

---

[3] Descartes, *Passions de l'âme,* §82; tr. vol. 1, p. 357.

provoke desire; as in the Cartesian situation, these objects are
worthy of their name, since between the thing used everyday, eventually useless, and the emblematic figure of a face,
or silhouette, or name (a "star"), the variation in occasions
for desire underscores accordingly the permanence of the
structure of passion that sustains desire. Lack of acquaintance
here becomes no longer an obstacle to passion, but its condition of possibility: it is necessary that objects be reduced at
once (prior to consumption) and especially (when they can
or must remain inconsumable) to their representation and
their image, so that they are able to offer themselves as
widely as may be wished to desires; this imaginary availability thus calls for a real unavailability. In the contemporary
explosion of eroticism, the most notable feature (and this is
what distinguishes it from such explosions in previous centuries, particularly in the nineteenth century) seems precisely
to be the absence of bodies, submerged by their image—an
abstract eroticism, an eroticism of the gaze, disincarnated.
We love by sight, just as one knows by sight, namely as one
"knows" when one does not know. Whence the obscurity
of bodies. Certainly, we have no trouble seeing objectifiable
bodies, consumed and caught in the sex trade, and soon, indeed, in the health trade; but such bodies become, within
this trade, substitutable, exchanged, replaced; they are not
able, and neither do they claim, to give body to anything at
all, other than a diffuse despair. For a body to give body, it is
not enough for one to be able to incorporate with him; it is
necessary that he himself assume a body, or better, that he
become incarnate. By incarnation we mean, following Husserl and without any direct relation to the like-named theological concept,[4] the possibility for a body of the world
(physical) to invest itself with the passive capacity for affection; what we wrongly name the body proper in fact designates the physical body (mine), which can affect itself with
(feel) another than itself. This body, alone, is worthy of the

---

[4] See the classic work of Didier Franck, *Chair et corps: Sur la phénoménologie de Husserl* (Paris: Editions de Minuit, 1981).

name flesh. And flesh is missing from the situation in which contemporaneity has placed love (or what stands for love). Bodies lack flesh, and this is why bodies cannot accede to any other whatsoever, nor propose themselves as real others—as bodies of flesh. Without flesh, no body can accede to love, for it remains unaffected by another person, or even any sort of other. Restricted to bodies without flesh, contemporary eroticism slides inevitably into solipsism, an eroticism without other.

The aporia in the first determination of love as a passion was predictable, moreover, by the simple fact that, from the outset, it has been deemed worthwhile to redouble it with a second determination: the intellectual love of God (Spinoza), rational love (Kant), and even *amor fati* (Nietzsche). This addition is worthy of acknowledgement. Yet for all of that, this second version will stumble immediately upon the contradiction of its formula. Intellectual love bears upon the rational object (the moral law, the substance) of a true, which is to say rational, idea. Union with or access to such an object by such means therefore necessarily takes place within the horizon of representation and of understanding. The will can come afterwards to ratify (Kant), but sometimes it disappears (Spinoza). Without any doubt this remains a doctrine of union with the sovereign good (or with whatever takes its place), but can we still qualify it as a doctrine of love? Is even an adequate representation sufficient to accede to something other than oneself, or even to another person? Does knowledge, even rational knowledge, allow union, or even more, love? On the contrary, can't we suspect that the privilege accorded to the rationality of the object (in order to surpass the first determination) annihilates all affection and all will?[5] In short, in order to produce a conceptual determination of

---

[5] We should not be too quick to invoke Kant here as a counter-example: the "holy will," which can alone put in motion the moral law, has the strange particularity of perhaps never being realized empirically; the Kantian doctrine can, then, deploy itself without in any way presupposing the will that nevertheless is supposed to assure its effectiveness. It may not be "hands" (Péguy) that Kantian morality lacks, so much as the will itself.

love, it is not sufficient to qualify as love the access to rationality by representation. Moreover, this second insufficiency
reappears in numerous forms of the common ideal: loves of
the truth (or simply of humanity, of justice, of the nation,
etc.) attain, in the best of cases, the rank of understanding of
the abstract universal, and the force of regulatory obligations.
Neither the one nor the other authorizes serious talk of love.

To talk of love, yet with seriousness: if the philosophical
division between these two loves prevents it, then doubtless
we ought to give up this approach. But in favor of what
other? Must we substitute a division between *eros* and *agapè*,
between self-respect (*l'amour propre*) and self-love, or self-respect and disinterested love, or something else entirely? One
can easily see that these dichotomies risk bringing us back—
with only slight shifts in position—to the dichotomy whose
aporia we have just sketched, and that every border traced
upon the heart of love, rather than being of service, wounds
it definitively. In order to emerge from this impasse, we will
therefore give up making distinctions in order to unite love
to itself, love to charity. And because love has also been distinguished from knowledge, we will attempt to think of love
itself as a knowledge—and a preeminent knowledge to boot.

III

Love knows. Not that it is always necessary to turn to love
in order to know the objects of representation (though in
many cases it is indeed necessary). But—and this will be my
thesis—only love opens up knowledge of the other as such.
By which, at an inevitable distance, it recovers the function
of charity.

As our starting point, let us take up the famous analysis of
intersubjectivity that Husserl set down definitively in the
fifth *Cartesian Meditation*. I, as transcendental subject, am
alone: I certainly have access, within the realm of reduction,
to objects through the intentionality that organizes my lived
experiences; but these objects remain simple objects, consti-

tuted through and through by my intentional consciousness, which gives them meaning; this meaning, like these objects, thus remains mine; in knowing them, I know other things than myself ("consciousness is consciousness of something [other than itself]"), but I do not know another I or alter ego. Is the solipsism thus reached unsurpassable? Husserl proposes a path for escape: a second reduction. If I consider myself alone, what do I have that belongs to me? Everything that is given strictly to me. But a new factor intervenes at this point: besides object intentionalities, my immanence attests a new phenomenon: my body. Or, more exactly, the extraordinary particularity that my body offers: it is the only physical (material) body that not only is able to feel aware of itself *(se sentir)*, but itself *feels (lui-même sente)*. My body has the status of flesh: it experiences, it feels, and it alone can do this; just as my hand feels and feels that it feels, my whole body feels aware of itself; and it achieves this because, more radically, it feels aware of itself, experiences itself, and affects itself first of all.[6] In the realm of the second reduction, the affections are given to me, along with my flesh; which is to say, I am given the very world that lies beyond the objects that I constitute. Now, in this enlarged world, I discover phenomena that behave as if they found themselves affected in the same manner as myself. In reasoning by analogy, I can suppose that they feel, experience, undergo affections, aim intentionally, constitute objects, and so forth. Respecting these analogies, I come to the conclusion that these phenomena, while remaining physical (material) bodies of the world, as such objectifiable, redouble themselves with flesh that feels and is affected. In this sense, by analogy to my "I" properly reduced, I see others appear in their incarnated bodies.

This phenomenological analysis, many times commented upon in opposing ways, certainly calls for in-depth discus-

---

[6] This last point was the remarkable achievement of Michel Henry, particularly in *L'essence de la manifestation* (Paris: Presses Universitaires de France, 1963 [1990]) and in *Phénoménologie matérielle* (Paris: Presses Universitaires de France, 1990).

sion—but we will not do that here. We must nevertheless underscore certain of its features.

(1) Husserl, despite his intention, does not end up with direct recognition of the other; the other's flesh in effect remains merely inferred from his visible behaviors, by analogy with my flesh and my behaviors: my flesh can feel the body of the other, who in return feels my flesh as a body, but I cannot directly feel if and how his flesh feels (and feels my flesh). Husserl often recognizes that the flesh of the other by principle remains foreign to me, without any intuition, appresented and never presented. How can this aporia be overcome?

(2) Instead and in the place of the lacking presentation of the flesh of the other, Husserl delivers only a new figure of objectivity: reasoning by analogy in effect allows me to confirm, verify, and complete my constitutions of objects (always limited to my intentional lived experiences) by others' constitutions of the assumedly same objects: our concomitant constitutive variations reinforce the objectivity of the objects. Husserl wrongly calls this operation intersubjectivity; in fact, it is only a matter of an intersubjectivity mediated by common objects, which would be better named an interobjectivity; moreover, it is this interobjectivity that, at least in principle, regulates the behaviors of the "scientific community" on the "universal campus." In any case, the effort to transcend the objectifying horizon of phenomenology in the direction of a horizon of nonobjectifying alterity collapses: even the other is inscribed within objectivity, though it be indirectly.

Because they remain strictly philosophical, these two objections have been made often, under this form or another. A third, less standard, objection can be added; I will privilege it because it opens a new path. Reasoning by analogy allows me to infer, from my own flesh, the flesh (though decidedly invisible) of another. Reasoning by analogy is justified, according to Husserl, by the concordances and correspondences between our two sets of flesh. This justification, however, justifies nothing, on several grounds.

(1) I could very well never find convincing correspondences, through inattention, through real incertitude, or through bad faith. We have only to recall the many debates, real or imaginary, over the humanity of "savages" and of primitive peoples, or even the souls of animals, to judge that the analogy between the flesh of the other and my own remains thoroughly problematic.

(2) Above all, facts have quite disgracefully established that one can refuse to accomplish the reasoning by analogy that Husserl calls for as a phenomenological formality: the extermination of the Jews and others rested expressly upon the denial of their status as flesh (refusal of the analogy), or, worse, upon the irrelevance of this very flesh to assure their status as other persons.

(3) There is no need, in any case, to appeal to these (exceptional?) extremes in order to invalidate reasoning by analogy; day in day out, we each experience its fragility; it is enough for us to admit that we do not recognize equally in every supposedly human body a flesh, or a fellow flesh, or a flesh that could be set alongside our own; daily life even frequently demands that we be economical in recognizing the bodies of others as flesh: working, moving about, doing business, and the like all require that I waste the least amount of time and attention possible in observing carefully whether the bodies that interfere with my own are worthy, or not, of the analogical status of flesh. There is nothing ordinary, economical or, therefore, uniformly exactable about the recognition of incarnation. From these multiple reasons for the same objection, we can thus conclude that reasoning by analogy infers the flesh (and thus the humanity, the personhood) of the other from my own flesh on only one condition—that I will it, and will it well.

What exactly is meant here by willing with a good will to recognize the flesh of the other? At the least this: the phenomenality of the other does not precede my (good) will with regard to him, but instead is its result. Or, again employing Kantian terms against Kant, one might say: I am able to treat the other always as an end and never as a means only if, first of all, I truly will that the other be for me another person—another man. Kant of course presupposes what is most aporetic (that I admit an other person, another myself) and passes over it in silence, in order to establish at length what is most evident (the universality and reciprocity of the "golden rule"). In short, in order for the other to appear to me, I must first love him. If phenomenology is able to lead up to this point, it does so only at its limit and aporia. Only a thinking of charity can advance further.

IV

Let us confine ourselves to sketching out some of the features of charity that allow it—and doubtless it alone—to give us knowledge of the other. For, when it is a question of knowing (and not merely experiencing) the other—the other *I* who, because just such, will never therefore become for me an available and constitutable object—it is necessary to resort to charity. Charity in effect becomes a means of knowledge when our concern is with the other, and no longer with objects (for which the evidence of the understanding suffices).

How do we distinguish the other from an object, supposing that we go about this conscientiously? By noting that the object regards us not, while the other does. The object certainly "regards" us, in the sense that it "concerns" us, and eventually becomes of interest to us, which is to say, is able even to arouse our desire. But regarding us in that sense only signifies that we feel the weight of our own interest weighing upon us, reflected back by the object upon which it exerts itself. We certainly take an interest in this object, but always through our desire with respect to it, so that we experience our desire reflected by it, more than we experience it itself; or rather this object is worthy of its name (that which opposes itself to us) only insofar as it reflects and sends back to us our desire. The object regards itself, but sends back to us only our own "regard," our own gaze, like a mirror (or, let us say, an idol). The other, in contrast, modifies from top to bottom the rules for the exercise of the gaze: he, and he alone, opposes a gaze to my gaze; he no longer passively reflects my gaze, like an eventually unfaithful object of my desire, but is always its faithful mirror; he responds to my gaze not with a reflection of my own, but with another gaze. The other, or the uncontrollable gaze. Most of the time, this experience befalls us as a trial, not only because we are talking about the slightly ridiculous situation found in bad detective novels ("I have the feeling someone is watching us"); rather, we are talking about the trial of discovering, within an official or unofficial gathering, that, among the numerous gazes that are listening to me (for the eye listens), there is one or more who pays attention to me in such a way that it is with respect to *them*, and no others, that I ask myself, "What do they think of what I am saying, or simply, What are they thinking?" What we call, a bit imprudently, a "love life" is born and in most case dies from this single question: "Why is it that he, or she, whose gaze weighs upon me, why is it that this gaze has become the constituting moment of my life?" In order for the other's gaze to arise, meddle with, and install itself in my consciousness, it is not enough for me to find myself standing before other gazes; everyday life accustoms me, without a doubt happily, to living before a crowd of other gazes, without any of them bothering me or taking hold of me; what is more, this life would become properly speaking unlivable if I had to envisage—or better: allow myself to envisage—every face that appears to me; most of the time, I do not see them, nor do I expose myself to them, but—as current speech has it—I simply come across them. To come across them means here to see them as simple objects (which they nonetheless are not), to be unaware of them as such, to hold to purely functional relations in regard to them: the unseen gaze of the employee, of the salesclerk, of the cop, and so forth.

How do we choose between these two attitudes? One could (and this was Sartre's accurate though characteristically hasty analysis) choose according to the following alternative:

either I exercise my gaze and the other thereby disappears into an object (café waiter, sadism, etc.), or the other exercises his gaze and I disappear, like a simple object (bad faith, masochism, etc.). In fact, though, the alternative unfolds rather differently: either I refuse the counter-gaze of the other and thereby hold him in place as an object (against Kant and Lévinas), or I accept not only the moral law and the face of the other, but above all that there is an other and that his counter-gaze is as valuable as my own. Such an acceptance is not automatic: the other has no power over me, except for violence, which, incidentally, I can exert against him, and which, as such, decides nothing. Nor does this acceptance result from the face of the other, precisely because its phenomenality depends upon the fact that I indeed will it. To accept the other's face, or better, to accept that I am dealing with an other (and not an object), a face (and not a spectacle), a counter-gaze (and not a reflection of my own), depends uniquely on my willing it so. What I will organizes itself into the following alternative: either I do not love him and I pass him by going around him (Luke 10:31–32); or I "approach him and, seeing him, am unsettled" (Luke 10:33). This alternative, this crisis, and this judgment determine either the appearing of the other, or his occultation. There is no other decision for such a determination. Friendship, the most carnal or the most sentimental love, and the most brutal desire, just like the most disinterested benevolence and the most perfect charity, play out only according to this singular game. Only this game can transform an object into a personal other, only this conversion of the gaze can give rise to the uncontrollable freedom of a counter-gaze, of another gaze, in short, of the gaze of the other person. Only charity (or however one would like to call it if one is afraid to acknowledge its name) opens the space where the gaze of the other can shine forth. The other appears only if I gratuitously give him the space in which to appear; and I have at my disposal no other space than my own; I must, then, "take what is mine" (John 16:15), take from myself, in order to open the space where the other may appear. It is up to me to set the stage for the other, not as an object that I hold under contract and whose play I thus direct, but as the uncontrollable, the unforeseeable, and the foreign stranger who will affect me, provoke me, and—possibly—love me. Love of the other repeats creation through the same withdrawal wherein God opens, to what is not, the right to be, and even the right to refuse Him. Charity empties its world of itself in order to make place there for what is unlike it, what does not thank it, what—possibly—does not love it. "I give you a new commandment: that you may love one another, that just as I have loved you, you too may love one another" (John 13:34). In what way does this commandment, habitually commented upon as an evidence, merit the title *new*? To begin with, its newness lies in the fact that here the love of neighbor no longer has anything natural, normal or spontaneous about it: to love others is commanded, and obedience here does not go without saying, precisely because it is being commanded. Next: because the reciprocity indicates that the counter-gaze, conceded gratuitously to the other, constitutes in no less a manner the condition of possibility of my own gaze. What is not included in the doctrine, to all appearances self-evident, of the unevenness between my gaze and the non-gaze of the other reduced to objectivity (Sartre), lies exactly in the fact that, if the other does not accept to gaze upon me, then I myself do not accede to the status of the gaze. A gaze is not truly accomplished unless, beyond objects, it sees a counter-gaze—which is to say, unless it sees a naught of object *(un néant d'objet)*, a pure invisible. For such is the final paradox: the gaze of the other is not seen, at least as an object; strictly speaking, it remains invisible—we do not look anyone in the whites of the eyes, but rather in the blackness and the emptiness of the pupil, in the only "spot" on their body where there is simply a void to see; we face up to the other in his gaze insofar as he remains invisible; but this invisibility, as such, reaches us more than everything of the other's that is visible; it is the other's invisibility that weighs on us, gazes upon us, and judges us, frees us or constrains us, in short, loves us or hates us. And it is this invisibility that we love or hate, because from the outset we have very much willed it, or not. And there is no other judgment, proximate or final.[7]

V

In order to approach the question of charity, it is above all important not to suffer the influence of what metaphysics has thought about love. For today, in this tradition, love and charity have suffered similar devaluation. Love is reduced to "making love," charity to "doing charity"—words prostituted in the first case, betrayed in the second, each equally submitted to the iron law of "making or doing," and thus of objectification. Faced with this disaster, theology finds itself put to the test: can it think anything about charity, without losing it immediately to the scorn in which the thought of our time holds it? Let us admit that often, the answer has been "no." And this deficit contributes more than a little, today, to the well-known crisis of speculative theology. The inaugural decisions to begin speculative theology over again, for and through faith (in particular in Barth and Bultmann), or for and through hope (think of Bloch and Moltmann), will lose their way if they are not extended by a decision in favor of and starting from charity. While awaiting this prospect, the only rule is doubtless never to weaken charity, and instead always to do it the kindness of supposing it the first among the virtues and the instance of grace. In particular, this rule advises postulating that charity is in no way irrational or merely affective, but that it promotes a knowledge; knowledge of a type that is doubtless absolutely particular, matchless, but knowledge nonetheless, because it has to do with "knowing the charity of Christ which surpasses all knowledge" (Ephesians 3:19). This hyperbole clearly does

---

[7] On this analysis, see Jean-Luc Marion, *Dieu sans l'être* (Paris: Presses Universitaires de France, 1991); *God Without Being,* tr. Thomas A. Carlson (Chicago: University of Chicago Press, 1991), chap. 1.

not imply the renunciation of knowledge, but on the contrary asks that we attempt to accede to a knowledge that *surpasses* our ordinary knowledge. What knowledge, then, if not the knowledge of that which does not depend upon the objectivity of the object: the knowledge of the other? To know following love, and to know what love itself reveals— Pascal called it the third order. In this context, the theology of charity could become the privileged pathway for responding to the aporia that, from Descartes to Lévinas, haunts modern philosophy—access to the other, the most faraway neighbor. It is doubtful that Christians, if they want seriously to contribute to the rationality of the world and manifest what has come to them, have anything better to do than to work in this vein.

August 1994

INDEX

INDEX TO BIBLICAL PASSAGES